THE LITTLE GREEN BOOK OF

GARDENING WISDOM

THE LITTLE GREEN BOOK OF
GARDENING WISDOM

Edited by Barbara Burn

Skyhorse Publishing

Skyhorse Publishing books may be purchased in bulk at special discounts for sales promotion, corporate gifts, fund-raising, or educational purposes. Special editions can also be created to specifications. For details, contact the Special Sales Department, Skyhorse Publishing 307 West 36th Street, 11th floor, New York, NY 10018, or info@skyhorsepublishing.com.

Skyhorse® and Skyhorse Publishing® are registered trademarks of Skyhorse Publishing, Inc.®, a Delaware corporation.

www.skyhorsepublishing.com

10 9 8 7 6 5 4 3 2 1

Library of Congress Cataloging-in-Publication Data is available on file.

ISBN: 978-1-62873-789-9

Printed in China

Photo Credits: Photographs were supplied by the institutions, organizations, or individuals credited below and are protected by copyright. Photographs not credited below were taken by the author. Mary Ballard: 92, 140, 144, 161, 175; Bartow-Pell Conservancy: 60; George Callas: 25; Mary Colby: 72, 90, 130, 137, 170; Michelle Miller: 52, 97; National Gallery of Art: xiv (Ailsa Mellon Bruce Collection, 1970, 17.54), 3 (Widener Collection, 1942.9.10), 11 (Gift of Victoria Nebeker Coberly, in memory of her son John W. Mudd, and Walter H. and Leonore Annenberg, 1970.17.54); Jane Protzman: 6, 9, 49, 58, 66, 68, 75, 79, 102, 108, 122, 126, 133, 152; Shutterstock: 14, 44, 47, 56, 85.

Contents

Contents

Acknowledgments

In putting together this little book of quotations about gardening, I naturally dove into innumerable books on the subject—some in my own collection, some in the collections of friends, and some on Google Books, an extremely useful resource that enabled me to check sources, correct erroneous transcriptions and attributions, and find new books I would not have found on my own. In particular, I would like to acknowledge the assistance of several friends who helped me along the way: Ellen Bruzelius, executive director of the Bartow-Pell Mansion Museum; Martina D'Alton, Mary Colby, Michelle Miller, Mary Ballard; Jane Protzman, and my editor, Steve Price.

Introduction

When I first began gathering tidbits of gardening lore for *The Little Green Book of Gardening Wisdom*, I was surprised to find there were so many quotes about gardening that deserved to be collected. Although I perused only a hundred or so volumes about gardening and agriculture out of the thousands that have been published since the invention of written language, I concluded that the subject of growing things was of far more universal interest than I had anticipated, and a great deal more uplifting than all the volumes devoted to war and political history. Indeed, many of the words devoted to the subjects of love and religion rarely conveyed attitudes as positive and generous as those demonstrated by gardeners toward other gardeners.

Historians have placed the beginnings of language and civilization with the development of agriculture, and it is fascinating to read about gardens of the Ancient Near East and archaic Greece, which are known to us today through cuneiform tablets and oral histories, later supplemented by texts in the Old Testament and eyewitness accounts from Xenophon, Diodorus, and other Greek and Roman historians. These gardens were not all created merely for growing food;

many were personal gardens designed to sustain the soul and please the eye (and nose). In these descriptions, you can follow the evolution of the Garden of Eden from Genesis into the *hortus conclusus* (enclosed garden) of the Middle Ages and eventually into the formal gardens of France in the seventeenth century and even the charming cottage gardens of England in the nineteenth century. And throughout that journey you will be able to see how the garden has represented for so many the connections between themselves and the natural world, the link with their gods, the bond to their fellow humans.

The most surprising part of my treasure hunt was learning that so many people known to us for their achievements in other fields were enthusiastic gardeners. Many literary figures, including Jane Austen, Edith Wharton, and Colette, were well known for their devotion to gardening, but that group also includes Edgar Allan Poe, Henry James, Rudyard Kipling, and Jamaica Kincaid. Philosophers from Socrates to John Locke to Ralph Waldo Emerson and politicians from Cicero to Andrew Marvell and Thomas Jefferson have all had wise words to share on the subject of man's relationship with the natural world through their gardening experience, along with such naturalists as the Comte de Buffon, Henry David Thoreau, and Edwin Way Teale.

The richest material, naturally, was provided by landscape and garden designers, from the personal gardens of Pliny the Elder and Gertrude Jekyll to the public spaces of Alexander Jackson Davis and Frederick Law Olmsted, and by amateur gardeners who have found fulfillment in the simple acts of digging, planting, weeding, and harvesting. It was refreshing to discover, as I read through garden history, how interconnected many of these writers were. The critic and artist John Ruskin was a great admirer of Homer's description of classical gardens in the *Odyssey,* and Frederick Law Olmsted, the designer of Central Park, among other masterpieces, admired Ruskin, as did Gertrude Jekyll, whose influence on flower gardening is still significant today. William Kent designed many important gardens in eighteenth-century England, virtually revolutionizing landscape design as he went, but he apparently had little to say on the subject. However, his friend the poet Alexander Pope, another devotee of Homer's garden descriptions, was able to put Kent's work into words when he wrote that "All gardening is landscape painting," and garden chronicler Horace Walpole praised Kent as an innovative genius who "saw that all nature was a garden." It is interesting to note that several writers on the subject of garden and landscape design were actually outspoken advocates of new ideas and tastes, choosing natural over formal approaches or dismissing annual beds in favor of perennial borders.

Another surprise for me was the large number of websites devoted to the subject of garden quotes, and at first I thought they would make my task easier, having captured many of the bits of garden wisdom handed down through the ages. In fact, however, these sites proved problematic, since most of them gave no sources for the quotes other than the name of those who presumably originated the phrases, and many of them contained quotes that were inaccurate or incorrectly attributed. I decided at the outset to restrict myself to using only those pieces of garden wisdom that could be traced to their origins, but instead of making my work more difficult, the chore in fact allowed me to find a great many bits of wisdom that the websites had missed.

Although there are many wise words in the pages that follow, there is not an overabundance of specific gardening advice, although most of the books on the subject, beginning in ancient Greece, were actually intended for use as how-to manuals. I put in a few bits of advice here and there, but my main criterion for inclusion here was the quality of the language, whether it was eloquent or straightforward, insightful or humorous. This is not a book that will give you useful pruning techniques or help you choose between a formal parterre and a colorful perennial border, but it will, I hope, give every reader a sense of comfort to know that we are not alone when we are down on our hands and knees fighting with weeds or planting a row of seeds that will one day bring us great pleasure.

A word about the organization of the this book: most subjects, including art of the garden, holy gardens, learning from the past, and design, seem to work best when the quotes are given in chronological order, but others, such as working the garden and plant selection, made more sense if arranged by subject rather than date. Readers looking for specific authors may find them in the index or the notes on selected writers.

One can experience wonder and delight in creating a garden, not just because others may admire our accomplishment or because it is inspiring to work successfully with nature to make something beautiful. As these writers tell us, the joy of gardening is the act itself—whether it involves using artistic talent to design a garden or doing the actual physical labor of preparing the soil and enabling the plants to fulfill their promise.

Barbara Burn
City Island, New York
September 2013

Camille Pissarro: *The Artist's Garden at Eragny.* 1898

CHAPTER 1

The Art of Gardening

[Gardening], too, is that kindliest of arts, which makes requital tenfold in kind for every work of the labourer. She is the sweet mistress who, with smile of welcome and outstretched hand, greets the approach of her devoted one, seeming to say, Take from me all thy heart's desire. She is the generous hostess; she keeps open house for the stranger. For where else, save in some happy rural seat of her devising, shall a man more cheerily cherish content in winter, with bubbling bath and blazing fire? Or where, save afield, in summer rest more sweetly, lulled by babbling streams, soft airs, and tender shades?
—XENOPHON, *OECUMENICUS* V (362 BC)

• • •

All art is but imitation of nature.
—SENECA, EPISTLE 65 (1ST CENTURY AD)

• • •

But Nature here hath been so free
As if she said leave this to me.
Art would more neatly have defac'd
What she had laid so sweetly wast;

1

In fragrant Gardens, shaddy Woods,
Deep Meadows, and transparent Floods.
—ANDREW MARVELL, *UPON APPLETON HOUSE* (EARLY 1650S)

• • •

All gardening is landscape-painting.
—ALEXANDER POPE, RESPONSE TO
JOSEPH SPENCE (AFTER 1727)

• • •

Landskip [landscape] should contain variety enough to form a picture upon canvas; and this is no bad test, as I think the landskip painter is the gardener's best designer. The eye requires a sort of balance here; but not so as to encroach upon probable nature. A wood, or hill, may balance a house or obelisk; for exactness would be displeasing.
—WILLIAM SHENSTONE, INTERVIEW (1746)

• • •

No occupation attaches a man more to his duty, than that of cultivating a taste in the fine arts: a just relish of what is beautiful, proper, elegant, and ornamental, in writing or painting, in architecture or gardening, is a fine preparation for the same just relish of these qualities in character and behavior.
—HENRY HOME, "BEAUTY," *ELEMENTS
OF CRITICISM*, VOL. 1 (1762)

• • •

John Constable: *Wivenhoe Park, Essex*, 1816

Gardening, in the perfection to which it has been lately brought in England, is entitled to a position of considerable rank among the liberal arts.

—THOMAS WHATELEY, *OBSERVATIONS ON MODERN GARDENING* (1770)

• • •

The Art of Gardening may be deemed the most useful and entertaining of all others, as it expands the variegated beauties of nature, and administers the most wholesome food to the body.

—SAMUEL COOK, *THE COMPLETE ENGLISH GARDENER, OR GARDENING MADE PERFECTLY EASY* (1780)

• • •

Painters and poets have had the credit of being reckoned the fathers of English gardening. . . . Laying out grounds may be considered a liberal art, in some sort like poetry and painting.

—WILLIAM WORDSWORTH, "OF BUILDING AND GARDENING AND LAYING OUT OF GROUNDS" (1805)

• • •

Nothing is more completely the child of art than a garden.

—SIR WALTER SCOTT, "ON LANDSCAPE GARDENING" (1828)

• • •

My long-stretching bean-rows, trim as an air-line, the peas binding the central wall and extending from the front gate to the brook, have a very pretty effect. . . . Nature! The outlines of all things and designs are drawn in Nature, and it is the sweet privilege of Man to divine and fill out these sketches, completing in Art what is begun in Nature. I think I garden more to the eye than to the appetite.

—AMOS BRONSON ALCOTT, JOURNALS (19TH CENTURY)

• • •

The development of the Beautiful is the aim and the end of Landscape Gardening, as it is of all other fine arts. The ancients sought to attain this by a studied and elegant regularity of design in their gardens; the moderns, by the creation and improvement of grounds which, though of limited extent, exhibit a highly graceful or picturesque epitome of natural beauty.

—ALEXANDER JACKSON DOWNING, *A TREATISE ON THE THEORY AND PRACTICE OF LANDSCAPE GARDENING, ADAPTED TO NORTH AMERICA* (1841)

• • •

True taste in the garden is, unhappily, much rarer than many people suppose. No amount of expense, rich collections, good cultivation, large gardens, and plenty of glass, will suffice. A garden of a few acres showing a real love of the beautiful in nature, as it can be illustrated in gardens, is rare; and when it is seen it is often rather the result of accident than of design.

A carefully landscaped home on the shore of Seattle, Washington

This is partly owing to the fact that the kind of knowledge one wants in order to form a really beautiful garden is very uncommon.

—WILLIAM ROBINSON, *THE WILD GARDEN* (1870)

• • •

What artist so noble as he, who, with far-reaching conception of beauty and designing-power, sketches the outlines, writes the colors, and directs the shadows, of a picture so great that Nature shall be employed upon it for generations, before the work he has arranged for her shall realize his intentions.

—FREDERICK LAW OLMSTED, *THE SPOILS OF THE PARK* (1882)

• • •

The gardener must follow the true artist, however modestly, in his respect for things as they are, in delight in natural form and beauty of flower and tree, if we are to be free from barren geometry, and if our gardens are ever to be true pictures. . . . And as the artist's work is to see for us and preserve in pictures some of the beauty of landscape, tree, or flower, so the garden-er's should be to keep for us as far as may be, in the fulness of their natural beauty, the living things themselves.

—WILLIAM ROBINSON, *THE ENGLISH FLOWER GARDEN* (1883)

• • •

In gardening, as in other matters, the true test of one's work is the measure of one's possibilities. A small, trim garden, like a sonnet, may contain the very soul of beauty. A small garden may be as truly admirable as a perfect song or painting.

—JOHN DANDO SEDDING, *GARDEN-CRAFT OLD AND NEW* (1891)

• • •

Flowers first broke up the prism and made the most subtle portion of our sight.

—MAURICE MAETERLINCK, *THE INTELLIGENCE OF THE FLOWERS* (1907)

• • •

It is just in the way it is done that lies the whole difference between commonplace gardening and gardening that may rightly claim to rank as a fine art. . . . In practice it is to place every plant or group of plants with such thoughtful care and definite intention that they shall form a part of a harmonious whole, and that successive portions, or in some cases, even single details, shall show a series of pictures.

—GERTRUDE JEKYLL, *COLOUR IN THE FLOWER GARDEN* (1908)

• • •

To make a great garden, one must have a great idea or a great opportunity.

—SIR GEORGE SITWELL, "ON THE MAKING OF GARDENS" (1909)

• • •

Not all gardens are in the ground.

Horticulture is, next to music, the most sensitive of the fine arts. Properly allied to Architecture, garden-making is as near as a man may get to the Divine functions.
—MAURICE HEWLETT, *OPEN COUNTRY:*
A COMEDY WITH A STING (1910)

• • •

In his garden every man may be his own artist without apology or explanation. . . . We may learn much of patience and tenderness, sincerity and thoroughness from these gardeners of other days and may well seek to endow our gardens with the restful charm of theirs, but we may fairly claim for our own day the great advance that has been made in the decorative employment of flowers—their arrangement and relation in the garden so as to bring about beautiful pictures.
—LOUISE BEEBE WILDER, *COLOUR IN MY GARDEN* (1918)

• • •

Apart from painting and gardening, I am good for nothing. My greatest masterpiece is my garden.
—CLAUDE MONET (EARLY 20TH CENTURY)

• • •

Every garden-maker should be an artist along his own lines. That is the only possible way to create a garden, irrespective of size or wealth.
—VITA SACKVILLE-WEST, COLUMN IN *THE OBSERVER* (1953)

• • •

Claude Monet: *The Japanese Footbridge*, 1899

You can make films or you can cultivate a garden. Both have as much claim to being called an art as a poem by Verlaine or a painting by Delacroix.
—JEAN RENOIR, *MY LIFE AND MY FILMS* (1974)

• • •

When we walk into a garden, we bring with us whatever delights we have seen in garden images: the dark, flower-strewn turf in Giovanni di Paolo's Paradise, the silvery shower of George Tice's New Jersey apple tree, a lacquer praying mantis looking for a foothold, or the splash of James Tissot's azaleas flood. . . . Memory and allusion augment the pleasures of the present. In turn, what we know of real gardens, their sights and smells, their history, the work and play we enjoy in them, informs and amplifies the marvelous images of all the green and flowery places we glimpse in works of art.
—MAC GRISWOLD, *PLEASURES OF THE GARDEN* (1987)

• • •

A garden will die with its owner, a garden will die with the death of the person who made it. . . . That very same garden that he (Monet) made does not exist; that garden died, too, the way gardens do when their creators and sustainers disappear. And yet the garden at Giverny that he (Monet) made is alive in the paintings.
—JAMAICA KINCAID, MY *GARDEN [BOOK]:* (1999)

• • •

Of course, in gardening we cannot reproduce Nature and, on the whole, it would not be desirable. Few people find beds of nettles or thickets of blackthorn attractive, even though they have their place in Nature's scheme of things and must be conserved where possible. We all find a haze of bluebells beneath beeches, primroses on clay soil beneath oaks or a damp meadow golden with buttercups more magical than anything we can create. However, in our gardens we look for more. We learn to make plant associations that extend the season, to create pictures worth living with throughout the year.

—BETH CHATTO, *DROUGHT RESISTANT PLANTING* (2000)

• • •

The enclosed garden of the Middle Ages, reflected in this herb garden at the Cloisters in New York City, is a direct descendant of the Garden of Eden.

CHAPTER 2

Holy Gardens

Your father, An the king, the lord who caused human seed to come forth and who placed all mankind on the earth, has laid upon you the guarding of the divine powers of heaven and earth, and has elevated you to be their prince. An, king of the gods, has instructed you to keep open the holy mouths of the Tigris and Euphrates, to fill them with splendour, to make the dense clouds release plentiful water and make them rain all over the fields, to make Ezina lift her head in the furrows, to make vegetation . . . in the desert, and to make orchards and gardens ripe with syrup and vines grow as tall as forests.

—SUMERIAN TEXT (3RD MILLENNIUM BC)

• • •

I give to thee great gardens, with trees and vines in the temple of Atuma, I give to thee lands with olive trees in the city of On. I have furnished them with gardeners, and many men to make ready oil of Egypt for kindling the lamps of thy noble temple. I give to thee trees and wood, date palms, incense, and lotus, rushes, grasses, and flowers of every land, to set before thy fair face.

—RAMESES III, ROYAL BENEFACTION TO THE
EGYPTIAN CITY OF HELIOPOLIS (12TH CENTURY BC)

• • •

And the Lord God planted a garden in Eden, in the east; and there he put the man whom he had formed. And out of the ground the Lord God made to grow every tree that is pleasant to the sight and good for food, the tree of life also in the midst of the garden, and the tree of the knowledge of good and evil. . . . The Lord God took the man and put him in the garden of Eden to till it and keep it. And the Lord God commanded the man, saying, "You may freely eat of every tree of the garden; but of the tree of the knowledge of good and evil you shall not eat, for in the day that you eat of it you shall die."

—GENESIS 2:8–9, 15–17

• • •

And God said, let the earth bring forth grass, the herb yielding seed, and the fruit tree yielding fruit after his kind, whose seed it in itself, upon the earth: and it was so.

—PSALM 104:14

• • •

To every thing there is a season
And a time to every purpose under the heaven;
A time to be born,
And a time to die;
A time to plant,
And a time to pluck up that which is planted.

—ECCLESIASTES 38:4

• • •

God made the earth yield healing herbs, which the prudent man should not neglect. . . . The essence of all beings is earth, the essence of the earth is water, the essence of water the plants, the essence of plants man.

—*CHANDOGYA UPANISHAD*
(BEFORE MIDDLE OF 1ST MILLENNIUM BC)

. . .

Another parable put he forth unto them, saying, The kingdom of heaven is like to a grain of mustard seed, which a man took, and sowed in his field: Which indeed is the least of all seeds: but when it is grown, it is the greatest among herbs, and becometh a tree, so that the birds of the air come and lodge in the branches thereof"

—MATTHEW 14:31–32

. . .

Gardening was a significant part of the early Christian monastery, serving as a spiritual refuge and an escape from besetting fears and doubts that assailed both the body and soul.

—WILLIAM HOWARD ADAMS, *NATURE PERFECTED:*
GARDENS THROUGH HISTORY (1991)

. . .

Allah has promised to the believing men and the believing women gardens, beneath which rivers flow, to abide in them, and goodly dwellings in gardens of perpetual abode; and best of all is Allah's goodly pleasure; that is the grand achievement.

—QUR'AN 9.72

• • •

Whereas those who believe and do right actions, such people are the Companions of the Garden, remaining in it timelessly, for ever.

—QUR'AN 25.82

• • •

What is Paradise? But a Garden, an Orchard of Trees and Herbs, full of pleasure, and nothing there but delights.

—WILLIAM LAWSON, *A NEW ORCHARD* (1618)

• • •

Flowers are the sweetest things God ever made and forgot to put a soul into.

—HENRY WARD BEECHER, *LIFE THOUGHTS* (1858)

• • •

A classic Islamic garden design, in which the central focus is water

Adam and Eve were put in possession of a truly botanic garden: God gave wild flowers as he made them, and left it with them and their successors in horticultural pursuits, to find their pleasure in making improvements. But . . . the efforts of man to improve certain flowers are futile.
—JOSEPH BRECK, *NEW BOOK OF FLOWERS* (1866)

• • •

If we could see the miracle of a single flower clearly, our whole life would change.
—AMOS BRONSON ALCOTT, *TABLETS* (1868)

• • •

Blessed be agriculture! if one does not have too much of it.
—CHARLES DUDLEY WARNER,
MY SUMMER IN A GARDEN (1870)

• • •

If we love Flowers, are we not "born again" every Day . . .
—EMILY DICKINSON,
LETTER TO MRS. GEORGE S. DICKERMAN (1886)

• • •

The lily was revered by the Greeks, who believed it sprouted from the milk of Hera, and Christians believe that white lilies symbolize the purity of the Virgin Mary.

There is an unerring rightness both in rude Nature and in garden grace, in the chartered liberty of the one, and the unchartered freedom of unadjusted things in the other. Blessed be both!
—JOHN DANDO SEDDING,
GARDEN-CRAFT OLD AND NEW (1891)

• • •

A garden is a lovesome thing, God wot!
Rose plot,
Fringed pool,
Ferned grot—
The veriest school
Of peace; and yet the fool
Contends that God is not—
Not God! in gardens! when the eve is cool?
Nay, but I have a sign;
'Tis very sure God walks in mine.
—THOMAS EDWARD BROWN, "MY GARDEN" (1893)

• • •

What is our love of flowers, our calm happiness in our gardens, but a dim recollection of our first home in paradise, and a yearning for the Land of Promise?
—SAMUEL REYNOLDS HOLE, *A BOOK ABOUT ROSES* (1896)

• • •

And he who makes a garden Works hand and hand with God.
　　—DOUGLAS MALLOCH, "WHOEVER MAKES
　　A GARDEN" (CA. 1900)

● ● ●

If you would have a lovely garden, you should live a lovely life.
　　—SHAKER SAYING

● ● ●

I think that if ever a mortal heard the voice of God it would be in a garden at the cool of the day.
　　F. FRANKFORT MOORE, A GARDEN OF PEACE (1919)

● ● ●

The best place to seek God is in a garden. You can dig for him there.
　　—GEORGE BERNARD SHAW, THE ADVENTURES OF
　　THE BLACK GIRL IN HER SEARCH FOR GOD, (1932)

● ● ●

For me different religions are beautiful flowers from the same garden or branches of the same majestic tree.

—MAHATMA GANDHI (20TH CENTURY)

• • •

In the creation of a garden, the architect invites the partnership of the Kingdom of Nature. In a beautiful garden, the majesty of nature is ever present, but it is nature reduced to human proportions and thus transformed into the most efficient haven against the aggressiveness of contemporary life.

—LUIS BARRAGÁN, OFFICIAL ADDRESS ACCEPTING
PRITZKER ARCHITECTURE PRIZE (1980)

• • •

I shall never have the garden I have in my mind, but that for me is the joy of it; certain things can never be realized and so all the more reason to attempt them. A garden, no matter how good it is, must never completely satisfy. The world as we know it, after all, began in a very good garden, a completely satisfying garden—Paradise—but after a while the owner and occupants wanted more.

—JAMAICA KINCAID, *MY GARDEN (BOOK):* (1999)

• • •

What turned wrong with Eden (from my point of view) is so familiar . . . and the caretakers, the occupants (Adam and then Eve) . . . seemed to have grown tired of the demands of the Gardener and most certainly of His ideas of what the garden ought to be, not so much how it ought to be arranged but whether its layout ought to remain intact, for this layout became boring to them after a while, this layout was not theirs, this layout (the Tree of Knowledge and the Tree of Life at its center) had all the sadness that comes with satisfaction.

—JAMAICA KINCAID, *MY GARDEN (BOOK):* (1999)

• • •

Why try to explain miracles to your kids when you can just have them plant a garden?

—ROBERT BRAULT, *ROBERTBRAULT.COM*

• • •

CHAPTER 3

Learning from the Past

For a history of a people's gardens is very nearly a history of the people themselves; and where civilization has maintained itself, there gardens have been made.

—GRACE TABOR, *OLD-FASHIONED GARDENING: A HISTORY AND A RECONSTRUCTION* (1913)

• • •

Our ancestors . . . were well aware of the cycle of the seasons and the recurrent labours which were appropriate to a particular time of the year. Before the twentieth century, the large majority of people still lived and worked on the land or were but a step removed from the patterns and rhythms of the countryside. Most of us today have lost that instinctive awareness of a continuous, cyclical development and pattern of change in the natural environment.

—JOHN FERGUSON AND BURKHARD MUCKE, *THE GARDENER'S YEAR* (1991)

• • •

Of all the implements, those used in gardening have changed the least. The hoe, equipped with a shell, antler, or animal scapula before the development of bronze or wrought iron, is prehistoric. Wooden rakes were known to the earliest Egyptians. Spades, sickles, pruning knives all are of extremely ancient origin.

—ELEANOR PERÉNYI, *GREEN THOUGHTS* (1981)

• • •

Everywhere the Persian king is zealously cared for, so that he may find gardens whenever he goes; their name is Paradise, and they are full of all things fair and good that the earth can bring forth. It is here that he spends the greatest part of his time, except when the season forbids.

—XENOPHON, *OECUMENICUS* V (CA. 362 BC)

• • •

Outside the gate of the outer court there is a large garden of about four acres with a wall all round it. It is full of beautiful trees—pears, pomegranates, and the most delicious apples. There are luscious figs also, and olives in full growth. The fruits never rot nor fail all the year round, neither winter nor summer, for the air is so soft that a new crop ripens before the old has dropped. . . . In the furthest part of the ground there are beautifully arranged beds of flowers that are in bloom all the year round. Two streams go through it, the one turned in ducts throughout the whole garden, while the other is carried under the ground of the outer court to the house itself, and the town's people draw water from it. Such, then, were the splendours with which the gods had endowed the house of King Alcinous.

—HOMER, ON THE PALACE OF ALCINOUS,

ODYSSEY (8TH CENTURY BC)

• • •

Talke of perfect happinesse or pleasure, and what place was so fit for that as the garden place wherein Adam was set to be the Herbarist? Whither did the Poets hunt for their sincere delights, but into the gardens of Alcinous, of Adonis, and the Orchards of the Hesperides? Where did they dreame that heaven should be, but in the pleasant garden of Elysium? Whither doe all men walke for their honest recreation, but thither where the earth hath most beneficially painted her face with flourishing colours?

—JOHN GERARD, *HERBALL* (1597)

• • •

The classical garden, in its symmetry reflects the influence of ancient Persia and the Near East described by Homer and Xenophon.

If we glance through the references to pleasant landscape which occur in . . . the Odyssey, we shall always be struck by this quiet subjection of their every feature to human service . . . Perhaps the spot intended . . . to be most perfect, may be the garden of Alcinous, where the principal ideas are, still more definitely, order, symmetry, and fruitfulness.

—JOHN RUSKIN, "OF CLASSICAL LANDSCAPE,"
MODERN PAINTERS, VOL. 3 (1856)

• • •

The beauties elicited by the ancient style of gardening were those of regularity, symmetry, and the display of labored art.

—ANDREW JACKSON DOWNING, *A TREATISE
ON THE THEORY AND PRACTICE OF LANDSCAPE
GARDENING, ADAPTED TO NORTH AMERICA* (1841)

• • •

Round her cave there was a thick wood of alder, poplar, and sweet-smelling cypress trees, wherein all kinds of great birds had built their nests—owls, hawks, and chattering sea-crows that occupy their business in the waters. A vine loaded with grapes was trained and grew luxuriantly about the mouth of the cave; there were also four running rills of water in channels cut pretty close together, and turned hither and thither so as to irrigate the beds of violets and luscious herbage over which they flowed. Even a god could not help being charmed with such a lovely spot. . . .

—HOMER, ON THE GARDEN OF
CALYPSO, *ODYSSEY* (8TH CENTURY BC)

• • •

Now and then a wearied king, or a tormented slave, found out where the true kingdoms of the world were, and possessed himself, in a furrow or two of garden ground, of a truly infinite dominion.

—JOHN RUSKIN, "THE MORAL OF LANDSCAPE,"
MODERN PAINTERS, VOL. 3 (1856)

• • •

The classic garden was an enclosed space protected from the outside world, a sanctuary from its clatter, frustrations, and woe. But it was also much more. It was perceived as paradise, the original paradise. Indeed, the Old Persian word *pairidaeza* means an enclosure, and the Greek word *paradeisos* means a garden.

—FREDERICK MCGOURTY, *THE PERENNIAL GARDENER* (1989)

• • •

The Garden was 100 feet long by 100 wide and built up in tiers so that it resembled a theater. Vaults had been constructed under the ascending terraces which carried the entire weight of the planted garden; the uppermost vault, which was seventy-five feet high, was the highest part of the garden, which, at this point, was on the same level as the city walls. The roofs of the vaults which supported the garden were constructed of stone beams some sixteen feet long, and over these were laid first a layer of reeds set in thick tar, then two courses of baked brick bonded by cement, and finally a covering of lead to prevent the moisture in the soil penetrating the roof. On top of this roof enough topsoil was heaped to allow the biggest trees to take root. The earth was leveled off and thickly planted with every kind of tree. And since the galleries projected one beyond the other, where they were sunlit, they contained conduits for the water which was raised by pumps in great abundance from the river, though no one outside could see it being done.

—DIODORUS SICULUS, ON THE HANGING GARDENS
OF BABYLON (1ST CENTURY BC)

• • •

[The dining room] looks upon the garden and the promenade which encloses the garden. This promenade is planted round with box, or with rosemary where the box fails; for box, when protected by buildings, grows freely; in the open air and exposed to the wind and the spray of the sea, even at a distance, it withers. Next to the promenade . . . is a plantation of young vines, affording shade, and soft and yielding to walk in, even with bare feet. The garden is clothed with a number of mulberry-trees and fig-trees—which the soil hereabouts is particularly productive of, while it is unfavourable to other kinds.

—PLINY THE ELDER, *LETTERS*, VOL. 2 (CA. AD 50)

• • •

Luxuriant grass, a fine plane-tree and a clear spring, hard by Ilissus, were inspiration enough for Socrates: in such a spot he could sit bantering Phaedrus, refuting Lysias, and invoking the Muses.

—LUCIAN OF SAMOSATA (CA. AD 145–60)

• • •

Plundering the past is by no means a new idea for gardeners. Both the Renaissance gardens and the eighteenth-century English landscape garden were attempts to re-create the village garden of classical antiquity.

—ROY STRONG, *SMALL PERIOD GARDENS* (1992)

• • •

If the medieval garden was designed to be looked down upon by the eye of God, its Renaissance successor found its optical focus in the eye of man. . . . This had a revolutionary impact on garden design, for instead of the garden being viewed in the medieval way as a series of isolated incidents, all of its ingredients were now marshaled in response to a single-point perspective, the rays of which converged in the eyes of the viewer. It was to be the greatest of all garden revolutions, for it gave rise to those elements which are still fundamental to garden-making today: vistas, avenues and cross-axes. These were used not only to divide a garden into geometric shapes on a grid system, but also to hold it together. . . . The medieval garden had been one of parts. The Renaissance garden, while still made up of parts, was conceived as a unity.

—ROY STRONG, *SMALL PERIOD GARDENS* (1992)

• • •

A typical European garden

The cult of the Italian garden has spread from England to America, and there is a general feeling that, by placing a marble bench here and a sun-dial there, Italian "effects" may be achieved. The results produced, even where much money and thought have been expended, are not altogether satisfactory; and some critics have thence inferred that the Italian garden is, so to speak, *untranslatable*, that it cannot be adequately rendered in another landscape and another age. . . . There is much to be learned from the old Italian gardens, and the first lesson is that, if they are to be a real inspiration, they must be copied, not in the letter but in the *spirit*. That is, a marble sarcophagus and a dozen twisted columns will not make an Italian garden; but a piece of ground laid out and planted on the principles of the old garden-craft will be, not indeed an Italian garden in the literal sense, but, what is far better, a garden as well adapted to its surroundings as were the models which inspired it.

—EDITH WHARTON,

ITALIAN VILLAS AND THEIR GARDENS (1905)

• • •

For a garden as a place of rest one must look farther afield to countries where a Moslem civilization has perpetuated an older tradition and design gardens for sitting in shade or sun, for listening to the song of birds and the plashing of water, and enjoying the scents of jasmine and rose and orange. . . . The tensions of modern life and an entire change in our ideas of scale and of speed have made physical tranquility a luxury.

—RUSSELL PAGE, *THE EDUCATION OF A GARDENER* (1962)

• • •

The symbolic value of the formal Islamic garden was as an earthly anticipation of paradise. In this sense, its contents of water, shade trees, and flowers were dictated by a generalized reaction to the desert environment, the traditional environment of Arabs, one that is dominated, of course, by aridity and conditioned by associations of the desert with fear and evil.

—THOMAS F. GLICK, *ISLAMIC AND CHRISTIAN SPAIN IN THE EARLY MIDDLE AGES* (2005)

• • •

On the subject of what must be taken into consideration in order to successfully find a location for a garden, a house or a farm [in Islamic Spain]: If you are considering a house surrounded by gardens, it should be situated on raised ground in order to facilitate guarding the house. The house should face the midday sun and be situated on the edge of the plot of land. The well and pond should be placed on the highest ground and even better just a well should be built, with a narrow canalisation flowing through the shaded parts of the land. . . . Near the pond, a stand of trees should be planted and maintained green for the pleasure of the eyes. A little further away, square plots of land should be reserved for flowers and evergreen trees. The property should be surrounded by vines and along the pathways arbours should be planted. The garden should be bordered by one of these paths in order to separate it from the rest of the property.

—IBN LUYUN, *TREATISE ON AGRICULTURE*
(FIRST HALF OF THE 14TH CENTURY)

• • •

Akikonomu's garden was full of such trees as in autumn-time turn to the deepest hue. The stream above the waterfall was cleared out and deepened to a considerable distance; and that the noise of the cascade might carry further, he set great boulders in mid-stream, against which the current crashed and broke. It so happened that, the season being far advanced, it was this part of the garden that was now seen at its best; here indeed was such beauty as far eclipsed the autumn splendour even of the forests near Oi, so famous for their autumn tints.

In the northeastern garden there was a cool spring, the neighborhood of which seemed likely to yield an agreeable refuge from the summer heat. In the borders near the house upon this side he planted Chinese bamboos, and a little further off, tall-stemmed forest-trees whose thick leaves roofed airy tunnels of shade, pleasant as those of the most lovely upland wood. This garden was fenced with hedges of the white deutzia flower, the orange tree "whose scent rewakes forgotten love," the briar-rose, and the giant peony; with many other sorts of bush and tall flower so skilfully spread about among them that neither spring nor autumn would ever lack in bravery.

—LADY MURASAKI, *TALE OF GENJI* (10TH CENTURY)

• • •

Recall the vistas of various famous places, select what attracts you and add your own interpretation. It is best to use this as a theme to design the whole of the garden while adding just the right amount of changes.

—SAKUTEIKI, *VISIONS OF THE JAPANESE GARDEN* (HEIAN PERIOD, 794–1184)

• • •

This Hawaiian garden borrows much from the Japanese approach to garden design.

Becoming more closely acquainted with things Japanese, I saw the native home in Japan as a supreme study in elimination— not only of dirt but the elimination of the insignificant. . . . For pleasure in all this human affair you couldn't tell where the garden leaves off and the garden begins. I soon ceased to try, too delighted with the problem to attempt to solve it. There are some things so perfect that nothing justifies such curiosity.

—FRANK LLOYD WRIGHT, *AN AUTOBIOGRAPHY* (1932)

• • •

Centuries ago, [the Japanese] developed a style of visual harmony through which the house with its furnishing, the garden, paintings, textiles, pots and pans were all made subject to an order of ideas.

—RUSSELL PAGE, *THE EDUCATION OF A GARDENER* (1962)

• • •

The "formal" style of gardening, reaching its climax in Le Notre's Versailles, had proudly imposed upon the infinity and irregularity of nature the finiteness and order of a little universe conceived by man—a universe cut out of (and off from) the great outdoors. . . .

—ERWIN PANOFSKY, "THE IDEOLOGICAL ANTECEDENTS OF THE ROLLS-ROYCE RADIATOR" (1962)

• • •

[T]he classic garden, that of Versailles in particular, has helped shape the contemporary reaction to the cataclysmic planning of the International Style by healing the wounds it has inflicted on our cities and knitting up the urban fabric once again.

—VINCENT SCULLY, *MODERN ARCHITECTURE AND OTHER ESSAYS* (2007)

• • •

Contemporary love of gardening in this urban century is a phenomenon that has spread widely, even though the threads that connect it with its historic roots are lost to all but the specialist. Even the simplest form of gardening is a particular kind of human experience that hints at a long and glorious past, both material and spiritual, but a sense of this continuity seems to elude us.

—WILLIAM HOWARD ADAMS, *NATURE PERFECTED: GARDENS THROUGH HISTORY* (1991)

• • •

The formal gardens at Versailles were designed by André Le Notre beginning in 1661.

CHAPTER 4

Design

Landscape Design

To build, to plant, whatever you intend,
To rear the column, or the arch to bend,
To swell the terrace, or to sink the grot;
In all, let Nature never be forgot.

—ALEXANDER POPE,
"AN EPISTLE TO LORD BURLINGTON" (1731)

• • •

Brute nature is hideous and dying; I, and I alone, can render
her pleasant and living. Let us drain these marshes, bring to life
these stagnant waters, by making them flow. . . . Soon, in place
of the reed and waterlily . . . we shall see the ranunculus and
the trefoil, sweet and healthful herbs. . . . A new Nature will be
shaped by our hands.

—COMTE DE BUFFON, *OEUVRES PHILOSOPHIQUES* (1753)

• • •

[On landscape designer William Kent]: He was painter enough to taste the charmes of landscape, bold and opinionative enough to dare and to dictate, and born with a genius to strike out a great system from the twilight of imperfect essay. He leaped the fence and saw that all nature was a garden.

—HORACE WALPOLE,
"HISTORY OF THE MODERN TASTE IN GARDENING" (1782)

• • •

[T]he good sense and good taste of this country will never be led to despise the comfort of a gravel walk, the delicious fragrance of a shrubbery, the soul-expanding delight of a wide extended prospect, or a view down a steep hill, because they are all subjects incapable of being painted.

—HUMPHRY REPTON, LETTER TO UVEDALE PRICE (1794)

• • •

The main theory and practice for [the English landscape garden] prescribed a three-step transition from form to formlessness. Near the house, in the foreground, the garden should follow a formal layout and thus be "beautiful." In the middle ground, the garden must be "picturesque" and, as the third step, in the background it must become "sublime" . . . not through the transition to formlessness and the unlimited sky, but rather by its being mere nature without any ruling.

—ALBERTO J. L. CARRILLO CANÁN, "THE GARDENS OF VERSAILLES AND THE SUBLIME," *ANALECTA HUSSERLIANA* (2003)

• • •

A view of the Blenheim palace grounds designed by the brilliant English landscape designer Lancelot "Capability" Brown, 1760s

The taste of the English in what is called landscape gardening is unrivalled: . . . the cherishing and training of some trees; . . . the nice distribution of flowers and plants of tender and graceful foliage; the introduction of a green slope of velvet turf; the partial opening of a peep of blue distance, or silver gleam of water.

—WASHINGTON IRVING,

THE SKETCHBOOK OF GEOFFREY CRAYON. GENT. (1819–20)

• • •

[Landscape gardening is] the Art of arranging the objects of Nature in such a manner as to form a consistent landscape . . . the art of hiding defects by interposing beauties . . . of contriving at every point some consistent beauty so that the imagination in every part of the theatre of his performance [i.e., the landscape] may revel in a continual dream of delight. [The landscape garden's] main object is to select from Nature all that is agreeable, and to reject or change every thing that is disagreeable.

—SAMUEL F. B. MORSE, *LECTURES ON THE AFFINITY OF*

PAINTING WITH THE OTHER FINE ARTS (1826)

• • •

[Landscape gardening] is an art which selects from natural materials that abound in any country its best sylvan features, and by giving them a better opportunity than they could otherwise obtain, brings about a higher beauty of development and more perfect expression than nature herself offers.

—ANDREW JACKSON DOWNING, *A TREATISE ON THE*

THEORY AND PRACTICE OF LANDSCAPE GARDENING,

ADAPTED TO NORTH AMERICA (1841)

• • •

There are, properly, but two styles of landscape-gardening, the natural and the artificial. One seeks to recall the original beauty of the country, by adapting its means to the surrounding scenery; cultivating trees in harmony with the hills or plain of the neighboring land; detecting and bringing into practice those nice relations of size, proportion and color which, hid from the common observer, are revealed everywhere to the experienced student of nature.

The result of the natural style of gardening, is seen rather in the absence of all defects and incongruities—in the prevalence of a beautiful harmony and order, than in the creation of any special wonders or miracles. The artificial style has as many varieties as there are different tastes to gratify. It has a certain general relation to the various styles of building. There are the stately avenues and retirements of Versailles; Italian terraces; and a various mixed old English style. . . . Whatever may be said against the abuses of the artificial landscape-gardening, a mixture of pure art in a garden scene, adds to it a great beauty. This is partly pleasing to the eye, by the show of order and design, and partly moral. . . . The slightest exhibition of art is an evidence of care and human interest.

—EDGAR ALLAN POE, *THE LANDSCAPE GARDEN* (1842)

• • •

Many a good house both old and new is marred by the vulgarity and stupidity of its garden.

—WILLIAM MORRIS, "GOSSIP ABOUT AN OLD HOUSE,"
THE QUEST (1895)

• • •

The Japanese, as you probably know, think that size in a garden does not matter, provided that everything is in proportion, and they produce the most wonderful effects of landscape gardening in a small space.

—GEORGE DILLSTONE, *THE PLANNING AND
PLANTING OF LITTLE GARDENS* (1920)

• • •

It is not difficult to plan an entirely new garden, but to remodel one that has had many hands on it is a far bigger task, like making over a dress, for one has to make the best of existing features, which perhaps cannot be removed, and can only be obviated by careful planning or building in vista.

—MRS. PHILIP MARTINEAU,
THE SECRETS OF MANY GARDENS (1924)

• • •

There is no garden so difficult to make well as an informal or wild garden, for absolute knowledge of technique and drawing is required, to quote painters' terms, and yet the whole effect when finished must be that of nature, unstudied and wild!

—MRS. PHILIP MARTINEAU,
THE SECRETS OF MANY GARDENS (1924)

• • •

A lovely border garden at Wave Hill in New York City

Surprise and hidden depths are part of the attribute of variety, whether it is the magnificently conceived hidden canal at Vaux or merely a curving path disappearing into the shadow of trees in a small private garden. A garden without mystery is not one to live with, although it may serve as a setting to some great building, to be seen purely as part of a view and not self as an environment.

—DAME SYLVIA CROWE, *GARDEN DESIGN* (1958)

• • •

To conceive of a garden as a piece of "nature unadorned" is of course a contradiction in terms. . . .

—ERWIN PANOFSKY, "THE IDEOLOGICAL ANTECEDENTS OF THE ROLLS-ROYCE RADIATOR" (1962)

• • •

To make a garden is to organize all the elements present and add fresh ones but first of all, I must absorb as best I can all that I see, the sky and the skyline, the soil, the colour of the grass and the shape and nature of the trees. Each half-mile of countryside has its own nature and every few yards is a reinterpretation.

—RUSSELL PAGE, *THE EDUCATION OF A GARDENER* (1962)

• • •

[M]inimalism in the landscape can ultimately achieve the visibility that allows humankind to celebrate—without irony and cynicism—the mystery, the essential *quidditas* of the physical world, the world we humans not only inhabit but of which we are only a part.

—PETER WALKER, *MINIMALIST GARDENS* (1996)

• • •

Garden Design

Four fundamental Maxims to be observ'd
Art must give place to nature.
Gardens should not be made dull and gloomy, by clouding them with Thickets and too much Cover. . . .
Gardens should not lay too open, so that it is needless to go into them. . . .
A Garden should always look bigger than it really is.

—JEAN BAPTISTE ALEXANDRE LE BLOND,
THE THEORY AND PRACTICE OF GARDENING (1712)

• • •

In laying out a garden, the first and chief thing to be considered is the genius of the place.

—ALEXANDER POPE, LETTER TO
THE PRINCESS OF WALES (1716)

• • •

The scenery of nature, called landscape, and that of a garden, are as different as their uses: one is to please the eye, the other is for the comfort and occupation of man."

—HUMPHRY REPTON, *FRAGMENTS ON LANDSCAPE GARDENING, WITH SOME REMARKS ON GRECIAN AND GOTHIC ARCHITECTURE* (1816)

• • •

Gardens are now treated like landscapes, the charms of which are not to be improved by any rules of art. . . . [T]o understand this style of garden requires a quick perception of the beauties of a landscape.

—ANDRÉ PARMENTIER, "LANDSCAPES AND PICTURESQUE GARDENS" (1828)

• • •

And now to sum up as to a garden. Large or small, it should look both orderly and rich. It should be well fenced from the outside world. It should by no means imitate either the willfulness or the wildness of Nature, but should look like a thing never to be seen except near a house.

—WILLIAM MORRIS, *MAKING THE BEST OF IT* (1879)

• • •

To the good gardener, all types of design are good if not against the site, soil, climate, or labours of his garden—a very important point the last.

—WILLIAM ROBINSON, *THE ENGLISH FLOWER GARDEN* (1883)

• • •

A typical Victorian cottage garden

Of all the things made by man for his pleasure, a flower garden has the least business to be ugly, barren, or stereotyped, because in it we may have the fairest of the earth's children in a living, ever-changeful state, and not, as in the other arts, mere representations of them. And yet we find in nearly every country place, pattern plans, conventional designs, and the garden robbed of all life and grace by setting out flowers in geometric ways.

—WILLIAM ROBINSON, *THE ENGLISH FLOWER GARDEN* (1883)

• • •

A garden rich in trees and shrubs, with ample breadth of well-kept lawn, will be enjoyable at all seasons without the aid of flowers. . . . Flowers alone do not constitute a garden; and when a garden has been provided to receive them, the display should be adapted in extent and character to the situation and its surroundings.

—JAMES SHIRLEY HIBBERD,
THE AMATEUR'S FLOWER GARDEN (1884)

• • •

In the teaching and practice of good gardening the fact can never be too persistently urged nor too trustfully accepted, that the best effects are accomplished by the simplest means.

—GERTRUDE JEKYLL, *SOME ENGLISH GARDENS* (1904)

• • •

The design of this garden in Maine is successful even without flowers.

The inherent beauty of the [Italian] garden lies in the grouping of its parts—in the converging lines of its long ilex-walks, the alternation of sunny open spaces with cool woodland shade, the proportion between terrace and bowling green, or between the height of a wall or the width of a path. None of these details was negligible to the landscape-architect of the Renaissance: he considered the distribution of shade and sunlight, of straight lines of masonry and rippled lines of foliage, as carefully as he weighed the relation of his whole composition to the scene about it.

—EDITH WHARTON,
ITALIAN VILLAS AND THEIR GARDENS (1905)

● ● ●

"We ascribe beauty to that which is simple; which has no superfluous parts; which exactly answers its end; which stands related to all things; which is the mean of many extremes." So wrote Emerson, with perhaps no dream of gardens in his philosophy. Nevertheless, in these words he gives expression to one of the most important principles governing successful garden design: simplicity. . . . No one in visiting a garden for the first time should be conscious that the design is good, but merely that it is a good garden. The garden does not exist for its design, but because of, sometimes in spite of, it.

—GEORGE DILLSTONE, *THE PLANNING AND*
PLANTING OF LITTLE GARDENS (1920)

● ● ●

This formal garden at the Bartow-Pell Mansion Museum in New York City reflects its European heritage.

Gardens have a terrible habit of getting too large, and need severe restriction. A garden to be beautiful and restful does not need too many flower beds.

—MRS. PHILIP MARTINEAU,
THE SECRETS OF MANY GARDENS (1924)

• • •

To me, hiring an interior decorator or landscape gardener is a little like learning fine sentences out of a book and using them when you talk. They may be much more elegant than any you could have thought up, but they are not you. Planning a garden is like planning a way of life; arrange it to please yourself, copying neither convention, nor tradition, nor any individual; enjoy it and hope that a few other people besides you will be pleased with it.

—RUTH STOUT, *HOW TO HAVE A GREEN THUMB
WITHOUT AN ACHING BACK* (1955)

• • •

Architecturally minded garden makers are apt to plan schemes which are satisfying and complete as constructions, but they sometimes seem to forget that a garden is a home for growing things and that a full planning scheme, laid over an elaborately architected framework, may add up to an indigestible whole.

—RUSSELL PAGE, *THE EDUCATION OF A GARDENER* (1962)

• • •

I have always tried to shape gardens each as a harmony, linking people to nature, house to landscape, the plant to its soil. This is a difficult standard to achieve and realization has always fallen far short of the concept. At each new attempt, I see that which is superfluous, that is, everything which clutters up my understanding of a problem must be discarded. Everything which detracts from the idea of a unity must go.

—RUSSELL PAGE, *THE EDUCATION OF A GARDENER* (1962)

• • •

A garden must combine the poetic and be mysterious with a feeling of serenity and joy.

—LUIS BARRAGÁN, OFFICIAL ADDRESS ACCEPTING
PRITZKER ARCHITECTURE PRIZE (1980)

• • •

The real aim of a garden is beauty, not low maintenance, but if we can attain a measure of beauty without spending all of our spare moments on weeding, pinching, staking, deadheading, spraying, encouraging, restraining, dividing, and conquering, we might have time to enjoy the garden more. Good design helps.

—FREDERICK MCGOURTY, *THE PERENNIAL GARDENER* (1989)

• • •

Like people, no two plots of earth are exactly the same. Each has its own personality, complete with strengths and weaknesses, and each will suggest its own garden design.

—KEN DRUSE, *THE NATURAL GARDEN* (1989)

• • •

Over the centuries, just what society has deemed to be perfection or even merely beauty in gardens has been subject to many shifts in taste and much impassioned, not to say dogmatic, argument. . . . In the process, the gardens of one era have repeatedly been plowed under to make way for the ideas or ideals of another. . . . Fortunately, all these narrowly focused approaches to gardening have faded along with the kind of aristocratic society that so long sustained them. In our more democratic times, gardeners feel free at last to borrow from many times and places or to be inventive in their own ways.

—WENDY B. MURPHY, *BEDS AND BORDERS:*
TRADITIONAL AND ORIGINAL GARDEN DESIGNS (1990)

• • •

Practical Design Advice

There are, however, some places of no great utility or fruitfulness but designed for pleasure . . . mainly for the delight of two senses, via sight and smell. They are therefore provided rather by removing what especially requires cultivation; for the sight is in no way so pleasantly refreshed as by fine and close grass kept short. . . . Upon the lawn too, against the heat of the sun, trees should be planted or vines trained.

—ALBERTUS MAGNUS, *DE VEGETABILIS ET PLANTIS*
[*ON VEGETABLES AND PLANTS*] (CA. 1260)

• • •

The ground is divided into beds, which, however, should be so contrived that the hands of those who weed them can easily reach the middle of their breadth, so that those who are going after weeds may not be forced to tread on the seedlings, but rather may make their way along paths and weed first one and then the other half of the bed.

—COLUMELLA, *DE RE RUSTICA* (1ST CENTURY AD)

• • •

In every garden four things are necessary to be provided for,— flowers, fruit, shade, and water; and whoever lays out a garden without all these must not pretend to any perfection. . . . The part of your garden next your house (besides the walks that go round it) should be a parterre for flowers, or grass-plots bordered with flowers; or if, according to the newest mode, it be cast all into grass-plots and gravel walks, the dryness of these should be relieved with fountains, and the plainness of those with statues; otherwise, if large, they have an ill effect upon the eye. However, the part next the house should be open, and no other fruit but upon the walls. If this take up one-half of the garden, the other should be fruit-trees, unless some grove for shade lie in the middle: if it take up a third part only, then the next third may be dwarf trees, and the last standard fruit; or else the second part fruit-trees, and the third all sorts of winter-greens, which provide for all seasons of the year.

—SIR WILLIAM TEMPLE, *UPON THE GARDENS OF EPICURUS,*
OR OF GARDENING IN THE YEAR 1685

• • •

A soft verdant lawn, a few forest or ornamental trees, well grouped, walks, and a few flowers, give universal pleasure; they contain in themselves, in fact, the basis of all our agreeable sensations in a landscape garden (natural beauty, and the recognition of art); and they are the most enduring sources of enjoyment in any place.

—ANDREW JACKSON DOWNING, *A TREATISE ON THE THEORY AND PRACTICE OF LANDSCAPE GARDENING, ADAPTED TO NORTH AMERICA* (1841)

• • •

What is the secret of the cottage garden's charm? Cottage gardeners are good to their plots, and in the course of years they make them fertile, and the shelter of the little house and hedge makes them fertile. But there is something more and it is the absence of any pretentious "plan" which lets the flowers tell their story to the heart. The walks are only what are needed, and so we see only the earth and its blossoms.

—WILLIAM ROBINSON, *THE ENGLISH FLOWER GARDEN* (1883)

• • •

I always think it desirable to group together flowers that bloom at the same time. It is impossible, and even undesirable, to have a garden in blossom all over, and groups of flower-beauty are all the more enjoyable for being more or less isolated by stretches of intervening greenery.

—GERTRUDE JEKYLL, *WOOD AND GARDEN* (1899)

• • •

A modest garden that reflects the simplicity of its cottage

The best situation for a garden is one that gets the morning sun, and is either right out in the open or sheltered on the north. It is best for the plants and best for you, because in a warm, sunny corner you can often work on days when it would not be safe in the chilly parts of the garden.

—CECILY ULLMANN SIDGWICK,
THE CHILDREN'S BOOK OF GARDENING (1909)

• • •

A rock garden, above all else, is not artificial; at least, so far as appearance goes. It is a garden with rocks. The rocks may be few or many, they may have been disposed by nature or the hand of man; but always the effect is naturalistic, if not actually natural. The rock garden's one and only creed is nature. . . . The advantages of a rock garden are, primarily, an element of picturesqueness that nothing else can provide, and the possession of a place in which can be grown some of the loveliest flowers on earth that, if they flourish at all, will never do as well in the ordinary garden as in conditions more or less approximating their natural habitat. Also it may be made a pleasance of extraordinary attractiveness.

—HENRY SHERMAN ADAMS, *MAKING A ROCK GARDEN* (1912)

• • •

Consult convenience in planning any sort of garden; it will insure fidelity to the spirit and letter of the old time as nothing else can for above all else the early garden makers here were practical, instinctively so. Their homes had to be productive, whatever the number of the slaves and however well they prospered, for that was part of their prosperity. Hence it follows that whatever they planned, they had always an eye to the care that must follow and to the ease with which that care might be insured.

—GRACE TABOR, *OLD-FASHIONED GARDENING:*
A HISTORY AND A RECONSTRUCTION (1913)

◆ ◆ ◆

It is now generally recognized that a rock garden should not have stones sticking up everywhere like a "garden sown with dragon's teeth," and that the rock should be subordinate to the flowers, used as a support to banks, as a ledge to be covered with creeping plants, or jutting out occasionally, as in a natural outcrop of stone, from among carpets of plants.

—MRS. PHILIP MARTINEAU,
THE SECRETS OF MANY GARDENS (1924)

● ● ●

Faced with a garden to design I have always tried to think about the shape it might take, of how I would want to move through the area, what existing features and what necessities such as circulation might be dealt with, and at the same time remain aware of the kind of plants I wanted or might need to use—for their forms, colours and textures would to a great extent influence the basic structure.

—RUSSELL PAGE, *THE EDUCATION OF A GARDENER* (1962)

• • •

In a narrow border too many tall plants will make it seem even narrower; in a broad expanse too many plants on a similar level give a flat two-dimensional effect. . . . A background hedge in a narrow border may give the desired architectural stability, its visual continuity and strong color framing the grouped plants in front of it . . . At the front of a border low planting with good evergreens will stability a scheme, linking a bed with lawn or pavement.

—PENELOPE HOBHOUSE, *COLOR IN YOUR GARDEN* (1985)

• • •

There is no rule that all of the elements of a border must be equally visible at one time. In fact, borders seen straight on, from a vantage point extending from the center, are often the least successful. If you can see everything as well from a distance, why bother to go closer?

—FREDERICK MCGOURTY, *THE PERENNIAL GARDENER* (1989)

• • •

Foliage combinations are more durable than floral ones because the leaves are present throughout the growing season.
—FREDERICK MCGOURTY,
THE PERENNIAL GARDENER (1989)

• • •

It is in July that you can assess the scheme. . . . Take quite detailed photographs for viewing when making alterations, and plan for next season's enjoyment.
—NATIONAL TRUST, *GARDENING TIPS* (1994)

• • •

Plant your perennials on paper before you put them in soil.
—HELEN VAN PELT WILSON,
THE NEW PERENNIALS PREFERRED (1991)

• • •

A well-designed garden looks as handsome in the fall and winter as in the spring.

Chapter 5

The Gardener

We come from the earth, We return to the earth, And in between we garden.

—AUTHOR UNKNOWN

• • •

I plant a garden for the householder. When the garden has been encircled, surrounded by mud walls and the agreements reached, people again take up a hoe. When a well has been dug, a water lift constructed and a water-hoist hung, I straighten the plots. I am the one who puts water in the plots. After I have made the apple-tree grow, it is I who bring forth its fruits. These fruits adorn the temples of the great gods: thus I enable the gardener to support his wife and children.

—SUMERIAN TEXT (3RD MILLENNIUM BC)

• • •

As the gardener, such is the garden.

—HEBREW PROVERB

• • •

He plants to benefit another generation.
—CAECILIUS STATIUS (2ND CENTURY BC)

• • •

The diligent farmer plants trees, of which he himself will never see the fruit.
—MARCUS TULLIUS CICERO (1ST CENTURY BC)

• • •

A Husbandman is the Maister of the earth, turning sterillitie and barrainenesse, into fruitfulnesse and increase.
—GERVASE MARKHAM, *THE ENGLISH HUSBANDMAN* (1613)

• • •

To prescribe one forme for every man to follow, were too great presumption and folly: for every man will please his owne fancie, according to the extent he designeth out for that purpose. . . . Let every man chuse which he liketh best.
—JOHN PARKINSON, *A GARDEN OF PLEASANT FLOWERS* (1629)

• • •

I never had any other desire so strong and so like to covetousness, as that one which I have had always, that I might be master at last of a small house and large garden.
—ABRAHAM COWLEY, *THE GARDEN* (1711)

• • •

A window box can be a satisfactory palette for a gardener who has no access to the land.

He who cultivates a garden, and brings to perfection flowers and fruits, cultivates and advances at the same time his own nature.

—EZRA WESTON, LECTURE AT
MASSACHUSETTS HORTICULTURAL SOCIETY (1845)

• • •

The first farmer was the first man, and all historic nobility rests on possession and use of land.

—RALPH WALDO EMERSON, "FARMING" (1870)

• • •

In his own garden every man may be his own artist without apology or explanation.

—LOUISE BEEBE WILDER, *COLOUR IN MY GARDEN* (1918)

• • •

Gardening or husbandry, and working in wood, are fit and healthy recreations for a man of study or business.

—JOHN LOCKE, *SOME THOUGHTS
CONCERNING EDUCATION* (1693)

• • •

There is not amongst Men a more laborious Life than is that of a good Gard'ner's.
—JOHN EVELYN, *KALENDARIUM HORTENSIS* (1664)

• • •

The athletic tend to look down on gardening—until they try it. Then I am amused to hear their moans and groans: "My *back*, I can't believe it." I can. I go through it every spring, and the cult of fitness has no part in my psychology. I loathe sport in nearly all its forms except horseback riding. But I figure my chances of a long life are at least as good as the average athlete's, and maybe a lot better.
—ELEANOR PERÉNYI, *GREEN THOUGHTS* (1981)

• • •

When all the chores are done, the avid gardener will invent some new ones.
—AUTHOR UNKNOWN

• • •

Earth, too, adds stimulus in war-time to earth's tillers; she pricks them on to aid the country under arms, and this she does by fostering her fruits in open field, the prize of valour for the mightiest. For this also is the art athletic, this of husbandry; as thereby men are fitted to run, and hurl the spear, and leap with the best.

—XENOPHON, *OECONOMICUS* V (CA. 362 BC)

• • •

As gardening has been the inclination of kings and the choice of philosophers, so it has been the common favourite of public and private men; a pleasure of the greatest and the care of the meanest; and, indeed, an employment and a possession for which no man is too high nor too low.

—SIR WILLIAM TEMPLE, *UPON THE GARDENS OF EPICURUS, OR OF GARDENING IN THE YEAR 1685*

• • •

I am one, you must know, who am looked upon as a humorist in gardening. I have several acres about my house, which I call my garden, and which a skilful gardener would not know what to call. It is a confusion of kitchen and parterre, orchard and flower-garden, which lie so mixed and interwoven with one another, that if a foreigner who had seen nothing of our country should be conveyed into my garden at his first landing, he would look upon it as a natural wilderness, and one of the uncultivated parts of our country.

—JOSEPH ADDISON, "GARDENS" IN *THE SPECTATOR* (1712)

• • •

This small town in Europe reflects the gardening impulse of its inhabitants.

Cultivators of the earth are the most valuable citizens. They are the most vigorous, the most independent, the most virtuous, and they are tied to their country and wedded to its liberty and interests by the most lasting bands.

—THOMAS JEFFERSON, LETTER TO JOHN JAY (1785)

• • •

When tillage begins, other arts follow. The farmers, therefore, are the founders of human civilization.

—DANIEL WEBSTER, *REMARKS ON AGRICULTURE* (1840)

• • •

And as the first man was shut out from the garden, in the cultivation of which no alloy was mixed with his happiness, the desire to return to it seems to be implanted by nature, more or less strongly, in every heart.

—ALEXANDER JACKSON DOWNING, *A TREATISE ON THE THEORY AND PRACTICE OF LANDSCAPE GARDENING, ADAPTED TO NORTH AMERICA* (1841)

• • •

How deeply seated in the human heart is the liking for gardens and gardening.

—ALEXANDER SMITH, *BOOKS AND GARDENS* (1863)

• • •

Little by little, even with other cares, the slowly but surely working poison of the garden-mania begins to stir in my long-sluggish veins.

—HENRY JAMES, LETTER TO ALICE JAMES (1898)

• • •

The true gardener loves his art so well that he will grow what he can even under difficult conditions.

—HENRY SHERMAN ADAMS, *MAKING A ROCK GARDEN* (1912)

• • •

To see another's garden may give us a keen perception of the richness or poverty of his personality, of his experiences and associations in life, and of his spiritual qualities.
—CHARLES DOWNING LAY, *A GARDEN BOOK* (1924)

• • •

Many a really fine gardener works for love of his profession, and, as a result, is not paid in proportion to his merit.
—MRS. PHILIP MARTINEAU,
THE SECRETS OF MANY GARDENS (1924)

• • •

The best policy for anyone new to gardening is to do his jobs by the calendar until he has built up sufficient confidence, experience and general understanding, to be able to break the rules cheerfully when it seems sensible and necessary to do so.
—CHRISTOPHER LLOYD, *THE WELL-TEMPERED GARDEN* (1978)

• • •

It usually starts with one plant. You are a nongardener until your Valentine gives you an azalea. Or your mother brings over a philodendron when you move into your new apartment. Or you go to the hospital with pneumonia and come back with a streptocarpus.

—BARBARA DAMROSCH, *THE GARDEN PRIMER* (1988)

• • •

Long ago I discovered that the plants I most enjoyed were those close to my comings and goings rather than those close to my sittings, since I don't seem to sit very much.

—HELEN VAN PELT WILSON,
THE NEW PERENNIALS PREFERRED (1992)

• • •

I have lived in three countries, but I feel that the immigrant and the gardener have this in common: long tap roots which seek nourishment deep beneath the surface of the earth.

—CARLA CARLISLE, *SOUTH-FACING SLOPE* (2001)

• • •

And he gave it for his opinion, "that whoever could make two ears of corn, or two blades of grass, to grow upon a spot of ground where only one grew before, would deserve better of mankind, and do more essential service to his country, than the whole race of politicians put together."

—JONATHAN SWIFT, *GULLIVER'S TRAVELS* (1726)

• • •

No occupation is so delightful to me as the culture of the earth, and no culture comparable to that of the garden. Such a variety of subjects, some one always coming to perfection, the failure of one thing repaired by the success of another, and instead of one harvest a continued one through the year. Under a total want of demand except for our family table, I am still devoted to the garden. But though an old man, I am but a young gardener.

—THOMAS JEFFERSON, LETTER TO CHARLES WILLSON PEALE (1811)

• • •

I had not set up to be a landscape-gardener before I came upon the [Central] Park. I had not thought myself one, and had been surprised and delighted when I was asked if I would accept even a journeyman's position in the intended word. Why? Simply because I held the art in such reverence, that, to that time, it had never occurred to me that I might rightly take upon myself the responsibilities of a principal in its public practice. My study of it had been wholly a study of love.

—FREDERICK LAW OLMSTED,

THE SPOILS OF THE PARK (1882)

• • •

Frederick Law Olmsted's love of the art of landscape gardening is beautifully expressed in his design of New York's Central Park.

Put an Englishman into the garden of Eden, and he would find fault with the whole blarsted consarn; put a Yankee in, and he would see where he could alter it to advantage; put an Irishman in, and he would want tew boss the thing; put a Dutchman in, and he would proceed tew plant it.

—HENRY WHEELER SHAW, *JOSH BILLINGS: HIZ SAYINGS* (1865)

• • •

Then seek your job with thankfulness and work till further orders,
If it's only netting strawberries or killing slugs on borders;
And when your back stops aching and your hands begin to harden,
You will find yourself a partner in the Glory of the Garden.

—RUDYARD KIPLING, "THE GLORY OF THE GARDEN" (1911)

• • •

A garden is always a series of losses set against a few triumphs, like life itself.

—MAY SARTON, *PLANT DREAMING DEEP* (1984)

• • •

'Eternal gardening is the price of liberty' is a motto that I should put over the gateway of my garden, if I had a gate. And yet it is not wholly true, for there is no liberty in gardening. The man who undertakes a garden is relentlessly pursued. He felicitates himself, that, when he gets it once planted, he will have a season of rest and of enjoyment in the sprouting and growing of his seeds. It is a green anticipation. He has planted seed that will keep him away nights; drive rest from his bones, and sleep from his pillow.
—CHARLES DUDLEY WARNER, *MY SUMMER IN A GARDEN* (1870)

• • •

Show me your garden and I shall tell you what you are.
—ALFRED AUSTIN, *THE GARDEN THAT I LOVE* (1905)

• • •

Some men like to make a little garden out of life
and walk down a path.
—JEAN ANOUILH, *THE LARK* (1952)

• • •

Naturally, every garden must be a law to itself. So much depends upon soil, aspect, and the taste of the owner. More depends upon his taste than upon his purse. A comforting reflection to end up on.
—VITA SACKVILLE-WEST, COLUMN IN *THE OBSERVER* (1955)

• • •

Growing things is like every other pleasure I have heard of: one enjoys it more keenly if one takes a rest from it.
—RUTH STOUT, *HOW TO HAVE A GREEN THUMB WITHOUT AN ACHING BACK* (1955)

● ● ●

Now the habits and patterns of our civilization impose a staccato and more shallow comprehension. There seems to be time only to look, note and look away. . . . It is a gardener's pleasure, as it could be the designer's privilege, to break this crazy rhythm to change and break the rush of time, and make the garden a quiet island in which a moment has a new meaning.
—RUSSELL PAGE, *THE EDUCATION OF A GARDENER* (1962)

● ● ●

As most gardeners will testify, the desire to make a garden is often followed by a desire to write down your experiences there—in a notebook, or a letter to a friend who gardens, or if, like me, you make your living by words, in a book. Writing and gardening, these two ways of rendering the world in rows, have a great deal in common. In my part of the country, there comes each year one long and occasionally fruitful season when gardening takes place strictly on paper and in the imagination.
—MICHAEL POLLAN, *SECOND NATURE: A GARDENER'S EDUCATION* (2003)

● ● ●

Where grows?—where grows it not? If vain our toil, We ought to blame the culture, not the soil.
—ALEXANDER POPE, *AN ESSAY ON MAN*, EPISTLE IV (1732–34)

• • •

Bad gardens are either mindless, or heartless, or both. I am not talking of flowers, even the finest flowers. That demands but little thinking, and no loving whatever. There is no more difficulty in having splendid-looking rose-blooms, or huge carnations, than in growing giant beetroot or colossal potatoes. But that is not gardening. Magical gardening is quite another matter.
—ALFRED AUSTIN, *THE GARDEN THAT I LOVE* (1894)

• • •

If man cheats the earth, the earth will cheat man.
—CHINESE PROVERB

• • •

Gardening gives one back a sense of proportion about everything—except itself.
—MAY SARTON, *PLANT DREAMING DEEP* (1968)

• • •

It takes a while to grasp that not all failures are self-imposed, the result of ignorance, carelessness or inexperience. It takes a while to grasp that a garden isn't a testing ground for character and to stop asking, what did I do wrong? Maybe nothing.

—ELEANOR PERÉNYI, *GREEN THOUGHTS* (1981)

• • •

How agitated I am when I am in the garden, and how happy I am to be so agitated. How vexed I often am when I am in the garden, and how happy I am to be so vexed. What to do? Nothing works just the way I thought it would, nothing looks just the way I had imagined it, and when sometimes it does look like what I had imagined . . . I am startled that my imagination is so ordinary.

—JAMAICA KINCAID, *MY GARDEN (BOOK)* (1999)

• • •

I am not a greedy person except about flowers and plants, and then I become fanatically greedy.

—MAY SARTON, *PLANT DREAMING DEEP* (1968)

• • •

There is nothing so terrible about not having a garden any more. The worrying thing would be if the future garden, whose reality is of no importance, were beyond my grasp.

—COLETTE, *EARTHLY PARADISE* (1966)

• • •

CHAPTER 6

Learning to Garden

Good gardening is very simple, really. You just have to think like a plant.
— BARBARA DAMROSCH, *THE GARDEN PRIMER* (1988)

• • •

Gardening, like other bents, will find a way but it will run more smoothly if it has a little help at the beginning.
— CECILY ULLMANN SIDGWICK,
THE CHILDREN'S BOOK OF GARDENING (1909)

• • •

And albeit she, good cateress, pours out her blessings upon us in abundance, yet she suffers not her gifts to be received effeminately, but inures her pensioners to suffer gladly summer's heat and winter's cold. Those that labour with their hands, the actual delvers of the soil, she trains in a wrestling school of her own, adding strength to strength; whilst those others whose devotion is confined to the overseeing eye and to studious thought, she makes more manly, rousing them with cock-crow, and compelling them to be up and doing in many a long day's march.
— XENOPHON, *OECUMENICUS* V (CA. 362 BC)

• • •

The more one gardens, the more one learns; And the more one learns, the more one realizes how little one knows.
—VITA SACKVILLE-WEST, COLUMN FOR *THE OBSERVER* (1950)

• • •

I would urge the reader to see as many different types of gardens as possible. Many a modest cottage garden has its lessons to give, and the observer will find them in strange places. Let him beware of public gardens and their influences; such as often a long way behind the time. The aim should be never to rest till the garden is a reflex of Nature in her fairest moods.
—WILLIAM ROBINSON, *THE ENGLISH FLOWER GARDEN* (1888)

• • •

But I have learned much, and am always learning, from other people's gardens, and the lesson I have learned most thoroughly is, never to say "I know"—there is so infinitely much to learn and the conditions of different gardens vary so greatly, even when soil and situation appear to be alike and they are in the same district. Nature is such a subtle chemist that one never knows what she is about, or what surprises she may have in store for us.
—GERTRUDE JEKYLL,
INTRODUCTORY TO *WOOD AND GARDEN* (1899)

• • •

One learns a lot by visiting other people's gardens.
—VITA SACKVILLE-WEST, *IN YOUR GARDEN* (1949)

• • •

This seaside garden requires a special approach to plant selection and arrangement.

Nothing is a better lesson in the knowledge of plants than to sit down in front of them, and handle them, and look them over just as carefully as possible; and in no way can such study be more pleasantly or conveniently carried on than by taking a light seat to the rock wall and giving plenty of time to each kind of little plant, examining it closely, and asking oneself and it. Why this? and Why that? especially if the first glance show two tufts, one with a better appearance than the other; not to stir from the place until one has found out why and how it is done, and all about it. Of course a friend who has already gone through it all can help on the lesson more quickly, but I doubt whether it is not best to do it all for oneself.

—GERTRUDE JEKYLL, *WALL AND WATER GARDENS* (1901)

• • •

If you have any good garden of hardy perennials within reach, you should visit it at different times of the year, and try to learn some lesson about the habit and arrangement of the plants. You will come back to your own garden in despair, but that is better for you than staying at home and being too easily satisfied. It is well to know the best that is done in any art or industry one tries to practise.

—CECILY ULLMANN SIDGWICK,
THE CHILDREN'S BOOK OF GARDENING (1909)

• • •

The good gardener is the one who makes experiments.

—VITA SACKVILLE-WEST, COLUMN FOR *THE OBSERVER* (1950)

• • •

This handsome perennial border serves as an inspiration to many gardeners.

A gardener learns more in the mistakes than in the successes.
—BARBARA DODGE BORLAND,
THIS IS THE WAY MY GARDEN GROWS (1986)

• • •

There is no gardening without humility. Nature is constantly sending even its oldest scholars to the bottom of the class for some egregious blunder.
—ALFRED AUSTIN, *THE GARDEN THAT I LOVE* (1894)

• • •

Gardening is an art that in the end must be largely learned by experience, and the earlier you begin to practise it the sooner you will find out some of the things all the books in the world cannot tell you.
—CECILY ULLMANN SIDGWICK,
THE CHILDREN'S BOOK OF GARDENING (1909)

• • •

Books teach much, and so also do lectures, but only when supplemented by practical experience will they make a competent gardener.
—FRANCES WOLSELEY, *GARDENING FOR WOMEN* (1908)

• • •

Reading is good but the garden is the best teacher.
—CHRISTINE ALLISON, *365 DAYS OF GARDENING* (1995)

• • •

Five minutes with someone who knows how to prune will teach you more than can ever be learned from a book.
—MRS. PHILIP MARTINEAU,
THE SECRETS OF MANY GARDENS (1924)

• • •

Gardening is like cooking: read the recipe and then use your head. A dash of skepticism can do no harm. Go lightly on caution, heavily on adventure, and see what comes out. If you make a mistake, what of it? That is one way to learn, and tomorrow is another day.
—RUTH STOUT, *HOW TO HAVE A GREEN THUMB WITHOUT AN ACHING BACK* (1955)

• • •

And a garden is a grand teacher. It teaches patience and careful watchfulness; it teaches industry and thrift; above all, it teaches entire trust.

—GERTRUDE JEKYLL,
INTRODUCTORY TO *WOOD AND GARDEN* (1899)

• • •

[M]y garden, like my life, seems, to me, every day to want correction.

—ALEXANDER POPE,
LETTER TO MR. ALLEN (1736)

• • •

The garden is growth and change and that means loss as well as constant new treasures to make up for a few disasters.

—MAY SARTON,
PLANT DREAMING DEEP (1968)

• • •

CHAPTER 7

Working in the Garden

When your field work becomes excessive, you should not neglect your work; no one should have to tell anyone else: "Do your field work!" When the constellations in the sky are right, do not be reluctant to take the oxen force to the field many times. The hoe should work everything.

—SUMERIAN TEXT

• • •

What is good cultivation? Good ploughing. What next? Ploughing. What third? Manuring.

—CATO THE ELDER, *DE AGRI CULTURA* (160 BC)

• • •

If you do not let laziness clog
Your labor, if you do not insult with misguided efforts
The garden's multifarious wealth, and if you do not
Refuse to harden or dirty your hands in the open air
Or to spread whole baskets of dung on the sun-parched soil—
Then, you may rest assured, your soil will not fail you.

—WALAFRID STRABO, *HORTULUS* (9TH CENTURY)

• • •

When man was first placed in the garden of Eden, he was put there . . . that he might cultivate it, which shows that man was not born to be idle.

—VOLTAIRE, *CANDIDE* (1759)

• • •

When I go into my garden with a spade, and dig a bed, I feel such an exhilaration and health that I discover that I have been defrauding myself all this time in letting others do for me what I should have done with my own hands.

—RALPH WALDO EMERSON, SPEECH (1841)

• • •

And I must work through months of toil,
And years of cultivation,
Upon my proper patch of soil
To grow my own plantation.
I'll take the showers as they fall,
I will not vex my bosom:
Enough if at the end of all
A little garden blossom.

—ALFRED, LORD TENNYSON, "AMPHION" (1842)

• • •

What a man needs in gardening is a cast-iron back,—with a hinge in it.

CHARLES DUDLEY WARREN, *MY SUMMER IN A GARDEN* (1870)

• • •

Our England is a garden, and such gardens are not made
By singing: "Oh, how beautiful" and sitting in the shade.
　　—RUDYARD KIPLING, "THE GLORY OF THE GARDEN" (1911)

• • •

If I have a spade . . . I can make the earth nice and soft and
dig up weeds. If I have seeds and can make flowers grow, the
garden won't be dead at all—it will come alive.
　　—FRANCES HODGSON BURNETT, *THE SECRET GARDEN* (1911)

• • •

Let no one think that real gardening is a bucolic and meditative
occupation. It is an insatiable passion, like everything else to
which a man gives his heart.
　　—KAREL ČAPEK, *THE GARDENER'S YEAR* (1931)

• • •

The best fertilizer is the gardener's shadow.
　　—AUTHOR UNKNOWN

• • •

In the spring, at the end of the day, you should smell like dirt.
　　—MARGARET ATWOOD, *BLUEBEARD'S EGG* (1983)

• • •

Being happy is dirt under your fingernails, wearing old clothes, having a good idea get better the longer you work at it, starting a new bed, giving plants away, and listening to rain.

—GEOFFREY B. CHARLESWORTH,
THE OPINIONATED GARDENER (1987)

• • •

Don't take on more than you have the time, money, strength or expertise to handle, either in the initial preparation or the yearly maintenance. I truly hope that you are not one of those people who, like me, believe they can do anything and must learn the hard way which things they cannot do, cannot do well, or refuse to do regularly.

—BARBARA DAMROSCH, *THE GARDEN PRIMER* (1988)

• • •

There can be no other occupation like gardening in which, if you were to creep up behind someone at their work, you would find them smiling.

—MIRABEL OSLER, *A GENTLE PLEA FOR CHAOS* (1989)

• • •

Make a New Year's resolution to plan better and so to work less in your garden. If you attempted too much last year, cut down. Gardens are not meant to be an endurance test but a joy.

—HELEN VAN PELT WILSON,
THE NEW PERENNIALS PREFERRED (1992)

• • •

Gardens are inherently artificial. Their spaces are artificially bounded; their elements are artificially selected and arranged; their appearance is artificially maintained. The universe naturally moves toward disorder, and gardeners must expend energy in working against this.

—MITRA K. MARTIN, "IN SEARCH OF PARADISE,"
ANALECTA HUSSERLIANA (2003)

• • •

Planting

Sow seed generously.
One for the rook, one for the crow,
One to die and one to grow.

—AUTHOR UNKNOWN

• • •

In seed time learn, in harvest teach, in winter enjoy.

—WILLIAM BLAKE, "PROVERBS OF HELL,"
THE MARRIAGE OF HEAVEN AND HELL (1793)

• • •

For man, autumn is a time of harvest, of gathering together. For nature, it is a time of sowing, of scattering abroad.

—EDWIN WAY TEALE, *AUTUMN ACROSS AMERICA* (1956)

• • •

Cristina, being something of a gardener, knew well enough that certain plants may appear to remain stationary for years while they are really making roots underground, only to break into surprising vigour overhead at a given moment.

—VITA SACKVILLE-WEST, *THE DARK ISLAND* (1934)

• • •

The commonest cause for the failure of seeds to germinate is planting them too deeply.

—RUTH STOUT, *HOW TO HAVE A GREEN THUMB WITHOUT AN ACHING BACK* (1953)

• • •

"Prove it for yourself," [John Lorenz] said. "Plant some carrots and beets the first of April and another row the first of May. Even if May doesn't exactly catch up with April, they'll turn out better, because they haven't been shivering the pep out of them for a month. They'll grow quicker, and anything is better if it grows fast."

—RUTH STOUT, *HOW TO HAVE A GREEN THUMB WITHOUT AN ACHING BACK* (1953)

• • •

There is nothing like the first hot days of spring when the gardener stops wondering if it's too soon to plant the dahlias and starts wondering if it's too late.

—HENRY MITCHELL, *THE ESSENTIAL EARTHMAN* (1981)

• • •

Lettuce is one of those wonderful plants that germinates quickly, giving encouragement to the gardener.

Too many of us start our gardening with seed packets. That's like concentrating on wallpaper and forgetting about the cellar. In gardens, as in houses, good foundations count, and a friable and fertile soil is the only sound basis for a beautiful garden.

—HELEN VAN PELT WILSON,
THE NEW PERENNIALS PREFERRED (1992)

• • •

Watering

As one who would water his garden leads a stream from some fountain over his plants, and all his ground-spade in hand he clears away the dams to free the channels, and the little stones run rolling round and round with the water as it goes merrily down the bank faster than the man can follow—even so did the river keep catching up with Achilles albeit he was a fleet runner, for the gods are stronger than men.

—HOMER, *ILIAD* (8TH CENTURY BC)

• • •

I would willingly drink myself, while the heavens are watering our fields. Come, wife, cook three measures of beans, adding to them a little wheat, and give us some figs. Syra! call Manes off the fields, 'tis impossible to prune the vine or to align the ridges, for the ground is too wet to-day.

—ARISTOPHANES, *PEACE* (421 BC)

• • •

Rain in the spring is as precious as oil.
—CHINESE PROVERB

• • •

An abundant supply of water, brought from the mountains by old Moorish aqueducts, circulates throughout the palace, supplying its baths and fish-pools, sparkling in jets within its halls, or murmuring in channels along the marble pavements. When it has paid its tribute to the royal pile, and visited its gardens and parterres, it flows down the long avenue leading to the city, tinkling in rills, gushing in fountains, and maintaining a perpetual verdure in those groves that embower and beautify the whole hill of the Alhambra.
—WASHINGTON IRVING,
TALES OF THE ALHAMBRA (1832)

• • •

God made rainy days so gardeners could get the housework done.
—AUTHOR UNKNOWN

• • •

You cannot give a recipe for watering as you can give one for a cake or a pudding, because the same plant will need different quantities in different conditions and at different times. . . . You know, of course, that plants must never be watered when the sun is on them. Nevertheless, if ever you see a plant flagging badly in the sun, and plainly dying for a drink, you may give it one carefully at its roots. Do not let the water touch its leaves, and, if possible, shade it for the rest of the day.

—CECILY ULLMANN SIDGWICK,
THE CHILDREN'S BOOK OF GARDENING (1909)

• • •

Water in the garden in any form is always an added delight, and there is now such a variety of plants suitable to grow therein at the command of a few shillings, that no one need be without them on the score of expense.

—GEORGE DILLSTONE, *THE PLANNING AND
PLANTING OF LITTLE GARDENS* (1920)

• • •

My thinking on the subject [of watering] is based on the assumption that water is our most precious commodity as the world population continues to explode, and modern demands for water are often in excess of actual need. Combine this with the likelihood of hotter and drier summers to come, then surely we must be prepared to reconsider some of our gardening practices.

—BETH CHATTO, *DEAR FRIEND AND GARDENER:
LETTERS ON LIFE AND GARDENING* (1998)

• • •

Pruning

Where economy of labour is essential, have some small patch of flowers quite near the house, small enough to be kept scrupulously tidy. It is so easy to put in a spare five minutes tying, weeding, pinching, or cutting off dead flowers while waiting for a telephone call or when a chance quarter of an hour's leisure turns up.

—MRS. PHILIP MARTINEAU,
THE SECRETS OF MANY GARDENS (1924)

• • •

Rose hips, a Poppy head, the satin of Honesty, the queer horned seed vessel of Love-in-a-Mist may be left where desired, but a safe general rule is to cut off dead blooms as often as you can find time for it; even so, there will be self-sown plants in many unexpected and often charming combinations.

—HELENA SWANWICK, *THE SMALL TOWN GARDEN* (1907)

• • •

Pruning is such a controversial subject that I approach it with diffidence, but of one thing I am sure: it pays always to clear the dead wood out of any shrub. . . . Take your saw and your secateurs, and give a breathing space, especially in the center. Let the light in, and the air. This advice is of general application, for there is no shrub that will not benefit.

—HELENA SWANWICK, *THE SMALL TOWN GARDEN* (1907)

• • •

Whatever you do about thinning, it is painful. If you pull out dozens of little growing plants and throw them away you feel like a minor murderer. But if you don't do that, if you plant some seeds and then, after they come up, you let them all waste their lives through your inability to destroy enough of them to give the rest a chance to grow up and amount to something, that is a sin against all of them.

—RUTH STOUT, *HOW TO HAVE A GREEN THUMB WITHOUT AN ACHING BACK* (1953)

• • •

Pruning, then, is as full of traps as of rewards. It is better to do none than the wrong kind. . . . I also strongly recommend discussing each [pruning] problem out loud with yourself or with the patient (let's call it, rather than victim). Don't be put off by silly people telling you that talking to yourself is the first sign of madness. Pruning calls for concentration and if you talk over the intricacies of the task, it will pass off all the more smoothly.

—CHRISTOPHER LLOYD, *THE WELL-TEMPERED GARDEN* (1978)

• • •

No plan which involves an expensive yearly effort on the same piece of ground can ever be satisfactory. All garden plants require attention, but they do not require this annually.

—WILLIAM ROBINSON, *THE ENGLISH FLOWER GARDEN* (1888)

• • •

This garden requires a good deal of pruning to keep its many shapes in rhythm.

Good grooming, you will discover, does as much for an out-of-bloom garden as it does for a plain woman.
—HELEN VAN PELT WILSON,
THE NEW PERENNIALS PREFERRED (1992)

• • •

There is nothing like pruning a grapevine for training oneself to think like a plant.
—HUGH JOHNSON, *PRINCIPLES OF GARDENING* (1997)

• • •

We say we love flowers, yet we pluck them. We say we love trees, yet we cut them down. And people still wonder why some are afraid when told they are loved.
—AUTHOR UNKNOWN

Weeding

When weeding, the best way to make sure you are removing a weed and not a valuable plant is to pull on it. If it comes out of the ground easily, it is a valuable plant.
—AUTHOR UNKNOWN

• • •

Now 'tis the spring, and weeds are shallow-rooted;
Suffer them now and they'll o'ergrow the garden.
—WILLIAM SHAKESPEARE, *KING HENRY VI, PART 2* (1596–99)

• • •

What is a weed? A plant whose virtues have not yet been dis-covered.
—RALPH WALDO EMERSON, *FORTUNE OF THE REPUBLIC* (1878)

• • •

We have found that a moderately sized plant of common groundsel produces about two thousand and three hundred seeds, that of a dandelion about two thousand and seven hundred, and that of the sow thistle about eleven thousand and two hundred. These are facts worth bearing in mind. Wage a constant war against all weeds.
—ROBERT ADAMSON, *THE COTTAGE GARDEN* (1856)

• • •

I have pretty much come to the conclusion that you have got to put your foot down in gardening. If I had actually taken counsel of my friends, I should not have had a thing growing in the garden to-day but weeds. And besides, while you are waiting, Nature does not wait. Her mind is made up. She knows just what she will raise; and she has an infinite variety of early and late. The most humiliating thing to me about a garden is the lesson it teaches of the inferiority of man. Nature is prompt, decided, inexhaustible. She thrusts up her plants with a vigor and freedom that I admire; and the more worthless the plant, the more rapid and splendid its growth. She is at it early and late, and all night; never tiring, not showing the least sign of exhaustion.
—CHARLES DUDLEY WARNER, *MY SUMMER IN A GARDEN* (1871)

• • •

Whosoever would sow must hoe. And if he who hoes would reap—he must weed. . . . Weeding is an art, though the back breaks. . . . But meanwhile weeds seemed fittest to survive in this unequal strife—in this contending, never-ending competition between Good and Evil or whatever the competition should be named.

—FRANK LLOYD WRIGHT, *AN AUTOBIOGRAPHY* (1932)

• • •

I feel that one of the secrets of good gardening is always to remove, ruthlessly, any plant one doesn't like. . . . Scrap what does not satisfy and replace it by something that will.

—VITA SACKVILLE WEST,
VITA SACKVILLE-WEST'S GARDEN BOOK (1968)

• • •

I never like to weed out anything that I can't identify. Not all seedlings are weeds. You may feel that life is too short to leave a seedling in till it's large enough to identify. My own feeling is that life's too interesting not to leave it there until you can identify it.

—CHRISTOPHER LLOYD, *THE WELL-TEMPERED GARDEN* (1973)

• • •

Unfortunately, in the very act of weeding, you make it possible for new weeds to grow. This is why mulching is so helpful.

—BARBARA DAMROSCH, *THE GARDEN PRIMER* (1988)

• • •

Mulching

It is a good plan, I think, to leave a heavy mulch of fallen leaves over the flowering shrubs instead of sweeping them all away. They serve the double purpose of providing protection against frost, and of eventually rotting down into the valuable humus that all plants need.

—HELENA SWANWICK, *THE SMALL TOWN GARDEN* (1907)

• • •

My way is unscientific, but it has produced fine vegetables for eleven years. I simply spread mulch where I want the compost to be eventually. It rots and becomes rich dirt, with the valuable by-products of keeping down weeds, keeping the earth soft, holding moisture and eliminating plowing and spading, hoeing and cultivating.

—RUTH STOUT, *HOW TO HAVE A GREEN THUMB*
WITHOUT AN ACHING BACK (1953)

• • •

Pests

The ditches of the garden should not flow with water, or there will be vermin.

—SUMERIAN PROVERB (3RD MILLENNIUM BC)

• • •

In order to destroy wasps, and other insects, which now devour the peaches, apricots, and other fruits, place phials of honey and ale near the trees, and you will soon catch large quantity of them. Renew the bottles once every week.

—SAMUEL COOKE, *THE COMPLETE ENGLISH GARDEN* (1780)

• • •

Is not disease the rule of existence? There is not a lily pad floating on the river but has been riddled by insects. Almost every shrub and tree has its gall, oftentimes esteemed its chief ornament and hardly to be distinguished from the fruit. If misery loves company, misery has company enough. Now, at midsummer, find me a perfect leaf or fruit.

—HENRY DAVID THOREAU, JOURNAL ENTRY (1851)

• • •

Pure soft water is the most potent of all insecticides.

—JAMES SHIRLEY HIBBERD,
THE AMATEUR'S FLOWER GARDEN (1884)

• • •

On every stem, on every leaf . . . and at the root of everything that grew, was a professional specialist in the shape of grub, caterpillar, aphis, or other expert, whose business it was to devour that particular part.

—OLIVER WENDELL HOLMES,
THE POET AT THE BREAK-FAST TABLE (1895)

• • •

The Garden! A comparatively peaceful place that Garden—when not raided by unnatural domesticated enemies from over the none-too-good fence—chickens, little pigs, and some few non-conformist sows. To say nothing of natural enemies underground—grubs, worms, and the marching armies of insects. Insects! Will they eventually win the battle and exterminate man?

—FRANK LLOYD WRIGHT, *AN AUTOBIOGRAPHY* (1932)

• • •

Of every single garden pest,
I think I hate the Green Fly best,
My hate for him is stern and strong;
I've hated him both loud and long. . . .

There was one Green Fly, I recall;
I hated him the most of all.
He sat upon my finest rose,
And put his finger to his nose.
Then sneered, and turned away his head
To bite my rose of royal red.

—REGINALD ARKELL,
"GREEN FLY," *GREEN FINGERS* (1936)

• • •

When I'm out working in the garden, running my hands through the soil, I forget, for the moment, about the cares and woes of modern life, and my mind drifts back over the years to biology class, when Mrs. Wright told us about these tiny parasitic worms that live in the dirt and get under your fingernails, and if you bite your nails, the worms get into your body and lay eggs in your muscles. I don't recall how serious a problem this was, but as a rule Mrs. Wright wouldn't discuss a parasite unless it was fatal. So Rule No. 1 of successful gardening is: Never bite your fingernails, or those of another gardener.

—DAVE BARRY
"GARDENING GROWS ON YOU," *CHICAGO TRIBUNE* (1985)

• • •

Harvesting

The thankful receiver bears a plentiful harvest.
—WILLIAM BLAKE, "PROVERBS OF HELL,"
THE MARRIAGE OF HEAVEN AND HELL (1793)

• • •

Earth is here so kind, that just tickle her with a hoe and she laughs with a harvest.
—DOUGLAS JERROLD, *A LAND OF PLENTY* (1859)

• • •

My garden is an honest place. Every tree and every vine are incapable of concealment, and tell after two or three months exactly what sort of treatment they have had.
—RALPH WALDO EMERSON, JOURNALS (1909–13)

• • •

Notwithstanding our disasters born of unseasonable frost and wet, sunless skies, I console myself with the reflection that on the whole we have made good progress. The garden is in better order than it was . . . last year.
—H. RIDER HAGGARD, *A GARDENER'S YEAR* (1905)

• • •

CHAPTER 8

Plant Selection

And because the Breath of Flowers is farre Sweeter in the Aire (where it comes and Goes, like the Warbling of Musick) than in the hand, therefore nothing is more fit for delight, than to know what be the Flowers and the Plants that doe best perfume the Aire.

—FRANCIS BACON, *OF GARDENS* (1625)

• • •

The true way to make gardens yield a return of beauty for the labour and skill given them is the permanent one. Choose a beautiful class of plants and select a place that will suit them, even as to their effect in the garden landscape. Let the plants be planted as permanently and as well as possible so that there will remain little to do for years.

—WILLIAM ROBINSON, *THE ENGLISH FLOWER GARDEN* (1883)

• • •

This handsome perennial garden serves to enhance the house it surrounds.

Though there be plants and flowers that are awkward or unlucky, there is none that is wholly devoid of wisdom and ingenuity. All exert themselves to accomplish their work, all have the magnificent ambition to overrun and conquer the surface of the globe by endlessly multiplying that form of existence which they represent. To attain this object, they have, because of the law that chains them to the soil, to overcome difficulties much greater than those opposed to the increase of the animals. And therefore the majority of them have recourse to combinations, to a machinery, to traps which . . . have often anticipated the inventions and acquirements of man.

—MAURICE MAETERLINCK,
THE INTELLIGENCE OF THE FLOWERS (1907)

• • •

I am strongly of an opinion that the possession of a quantity of plants, however, good the plants may be themselves and however ample their number, does not make a garden; it only makes a collection. Having got the plants, the great thing is to use them with careful selection and definite intentions. . . . It seems to me that the duty we owe to our gardens and to our own bettering in our gardens is to use the plants that they shall form beautiful pictures; and that, while delighting our eyes, they should be always training those eyes to a more exalted criticism.

—GERTRUDE JEKYLL, *COLOUR SCHEMES*
FOR THE FLOWER GARDEN (1908)

• • •

I would counsel buying or growing more plants than you need and keeping a few by to cope with disasters.

—ROY STRONG, *SMALL PERIOD GARDENS* (1988)

• • •

Three fundamental aspects of border design—site, shape, and size—have at least as great an effect on the ease of garden maintenance as does the actual selection of plants.

—FREDERICK MCGOURTY,
THE PERENNIAL GARDENER (1989)

• • •

Like people, perennials have their limitations. Until we allow for these, while emphasizing all their glorious assets, we can never create pictures which quite suit us. We must eventually admit, therefore, that a satisfactory border starts not with seeds, soil or plants but with the gardener's state of mind. It is, in fact, an exercise in evaluation.

—HELEN VAN PELT WILSON,
THE NEW PERENNIALS PREFERRED (1992)

• • •

Color

When daisies pied and violets blue,
And lady-smocks all silver white
And Cuckoo-buds of yellow hue
Do paint the meadows with delight.

—WILLIAM SHAKESPEARE, SONG FROM
LOVE'S LABOURS LOST (1594–95)

• • •

On the whole, I think the best and safest plan is to mix up your flowers, and rather eschew great masses of colour—in combination, I mean. But there are some flowers which are bad colour altogether, and not to be used at all. Scarlet geraniums, for instance, or the yellow calceolaria, which indeed are not uncommonly grown together profusely, in order, I suppose, to show that even flowers can be thoroughly ugly.

—WILLIAM MORRIS, "MAKING THE BEST OF IT" (1879)

• • •

The way colour is applied in brilliant flowers is the subject of a never-ending and always delightful investigation. All painters know how difficult it is to get a brilliant colouring of clear, unmuddled scarlet. It can only be done, especially in water-colour, by running the scarlet over a preparation of clear strong yellow. This is exactly how nature gets over the same difficult in flowers of that colour.

—GERTRUDE JEKYLL, *HOME AND GARDEN* (1901)

• • •

It is a curious thing that people will sometimes spoil some garden project for the sake of a word. For instance a blue garden, for beauty's sake, may be hungering for a group of white lilies, or something of the palest lemon-yellow, but is not allowed to have it because it is called the blue garden, and there must be no other flowers. Any experienced colorist knows that the blues will be more telling—more purely blue—by the juxtaposition of rightly placed complementary color.

—GERTRUDE JEKYLL,
COLOUR IN THE FLOWER GARDEN (1908)

• • •

It is true that in the natural progress of the seasons we have certain colours predominating at certain periods. The earliest colour scheme of the garden, as of the world beyond its walls, is yellow and white; this is followed by the rose colour of late spring and early summer when fruit blossoms and then Roses adorn the world. Next come the blue and yellow of midsummer which deepen to scarlet, gold, and purple as autumn lavishly spreads the colours. This natural scheme of colour we may modify or accentuate as often as we like, but to choose it as a sort of underlying theme much simplifies our work, since there are always plenty of good and willing flowers decked in the prevailing colours of the season.

—LOUISE BEEBE WILDER,
COLOUR IN MY GARDEN (1918)

• • •

In the most beautiful landscape the richest and most vivid colour is always in the foreground, and fades in tone in the middle distance, and the eye loses itself in the distance in indefinite purple and grey, and it is, in effect, this idea that is aimed at in the graduated colour border.

—GEORGE DILLSTONE, *THE PLANNING AND PLANTING OF LITTLE GARDENS* (1920)

• • •

As regards colour, remember that the simpler the treatment, the more effective. Large beds and stretches of cloudy blue forget-me-nots set in green turf and with fresh spring foliage and the stems of trees as a background is a delightful and satisfying picture. The same beds spotted with tulips in various shades and with a few beds of wallflowers and mauve aubrietia become almost vulgar. The chief reason that daffodils are so universally admired all planted in masses is, I am sure, that they are all one colour and it is this stretch of a simple colour which fills the eye.

—MRS. PHILIP MARTINEAU, *THE SECRETS OF MANY GARDENS* (1924)

• • •

A sameness of colour makes a dull garden. Nature loves a patchwork or kaleidoscope effect, and the best spring gardens are nearly always those where several colours are judiciously blended.

—MRS. PHILIP MARTINEAU, *THE SECRETS OF MANY GARDENS* (1924)

• • •

For a tiny garden, this has a remarkable array of colors.

It is amusing to make one-colour gardens. . . . The site chosen must depend upon the general lay-out, the size of the garden, and the opportunities offered. And if you think that one colour would be monotonous, you can have a two- or even a three-colour, provided the colours are happily married, which is sometimes easier of achievement in the vegetable than in the human world. You can have, for instance, the blues and the purples, or the yellows and the bronzes, with their attendant mauves and orange, respectively. Personal taste alone will dictate what you choose. For my own part, I am trying to make a grey, green, and white garden. This is an experiment which I ardently hope may be successful, though I doubt it. One's best ideas seldom play up in practice to one's expectations, especially in gardening, where everything looks so well on paper and in the catalogues, but fails so lamentably in fulfilment after you have tucked your plans into the soil. Still, one hopes.

—VITA SACKVILLE-WEST, COLUMN IN *THE OBSERVER* (1950)

• • •

The longer I garden, the more strongly it is borne in upon me that the contrasting of complementary colours, such as blue with yellow or pink with grey, is no worthier an object than the association of colours that are near to and distinct, one from another. . . . If we have our yellow sunflowers, golden rods, yarrows and ragworts all mixed up with phloxes, hydrangeas and michaelmas daisies, we shall get terribly self-conscious about balance and the quarrelsome overbearingness of yellow. But if we get all the yellows, including also cream, together, most of these worries will simply melt away.

—CHRISTOPHER LLOYD, *THE WELL-TEMPERED GARDEN* (1973)

• • •

A single-color Swiss garden

Many garden visitors notice only the eye-catching hues: I believe that, stimulating as these are, the more subdued effects and the background greens and grays are also worth studying. What is inspiring is ultimately a question of personal vision and taste, and I am naturally drawn to recommend the types of garden that seem to me to use color most excitingly. But a word of warning, perhaps most simply summed up by the formula "Avoid using *too much* color." This is the impression given when colors are not set into the green or gray framework that holds a design together, and is even more applicable to colored foliage than to flower colors.

—PENELOPE HOBHOUSE, *COLOR IN YOUR GARDEN* (1985)

• • •

[The gardener] cannot change colors by mixing pigments as the painter does, but like the painter he will affect the appearance of a color by where he places it. No color is seen in isolation; each is perceived in relation to some other color or colors and is constantly modified not only by its neighbors but by *all* colors immediately visible at a glance, and by those which were seen a moment before.

—PENELOPE HOBHOUSE, *COLOR IN YOUR GARDEN* (1985)

• • •

The garden in early spring might well be inspired by Nature's own design: trees and shrubs flowering in clouds of white blossoms with an occasional pink or delicate rose-coloured shrub blended in, to give a tempered warmth to what might otherwise be too frosty a picture.

—JOHN FERGUSON AND BURKHARD MUCKE,
THE GARDENER'S YEAR (1991)

• • •

A brilliant combination of greens

You can easily make your own scheme—and indeed change it from year to year in terms of both colour and plants—keeping to certain guide lines: the border plants should be low, those within the beds should be of equal height; no earth should be visible; introduce one or more vertical accents; bank up the beds, especially at the centre; aim for colour balance, but not in mirror image terms; and never place yellow at the centre.
—ROY STRONG, *SMALL PERIOD GARDENS* (1992)

• • •

Flowers

I will not enter upon any account of flowers, having only pleased myself with seeing or smelling them, and not troubled myself with the care, which is more the ladies' part than the men's; but the success is wholly in the gardener.
—SIR WILLIAM TEMPLE, *UPON THE GARDENS
OF EPICURUS, OR OF GARDENING IN THE YEAR 1685*

• • •

To create a little flower is the labour of ages.
—WILLIAM BLAKE, "PROVERBS OF HELL,"
THE MARRIAGE OF HEAVEN AND HELL (1793)

• • •

Give me odorous at sunrise a garden of beautiful flowers where I can walk undisturb'd.

—WALT WHITMAN,
"GIVE ME THE SPLENDID SILENT SUN" (1865)

• • •

The bedding system is an embellishment added to the garden; the herbaceous border is a necessary fundamental feature.

—JAMES SHIRLEY HIBBERD,
THE AMATEUR'S FLOWER GARDEN (1884)

• • •

Annuals as a class are not desirable for the rock garden; for one thing, the care of renewal is too great. Biennials are almost as much care, but in each case there will always be exceptions that are a matter of individual preference. Few, for example, would have the heart to reject the dainty little purple toadflax of Switzerland (*Linaria alpina*), just because it is a biennial. The main dependence, however, must be placed on perennials—the plants that, barring accidents, last indefinitely.

—HENRY SHERMAN ADAMS, *MAKING A ROCK GARDEN* (1912)

• • •

It took me time to understand my waterlilies. I had planted them for the pleasure of it; I grew them without ever thinking of painting them.

—CLAUDE MONET, QUOTED ON *WWW.CLAUDE-MONET.COM*

• • •

There is no guarantee that the flowers I have chosen would flatter the eye when assembled. Besides, there are others I can't call to mind at the moment. But there's no hurry. I shall dig them all into their storage trenches, some in my memory, the others in my imagination. There, thanks be to God, they can still find the humus, the slightly bitter water, the warmth and the gratitude which will perhaps keep them from dying.

—COLETTE, *EARTHLY PARADISE* (1966)

• • •

Perennials are the ones that grow like weeds, biennials are the ones that die this year instead of next, and hardy annuals are the ones that never come up at all.

—KATHERINE WHITEHORN, *OBSERVATIONS* (1970)

• • •

Plants that flower, set seed and die within a single season, they can perform prodigies in their brief lives.

—ELEANOR PERÉNYI, *GREEN THOUGHTS* (1981)

• • •

It is better to look to annuals not so much for vivid color accompaniments for perennial gardens, but for those traits that are a bit short in perennialdom.

—FREDERICK MCGOURTY, *THE PERENNIAL GARDENER* (1989)

• • •

Do the antiques have a place in modern gardens? They probably don't for many people, but for others, the charm of simplicity, durability, and often fragrance is important. . . . This is not to say that the old-timers are necessarily better garden plants (some obviously are not), but in many cases they will be around long after many thoroughbred cultivars of today have been forgotten. And there is a certain innate pleasure in growing—and enjoying—the same plants our forebears did.

—FREDERICK MCGOURTY,
THE PERENNIAL GARDENER (1989)

• • •

Fruit Trees

Pear grows on pear, apple on apple, and fig on fig, and so also with the grapes, for there is an excellent vineyard: on the level ground of a part of this, the grapes are being made into raisins; in another part they are being gathered; some are being trodden in the wine tubs, others further on have shed their blossom and are beginning to show fruit, others again are just changing colour.

—HOMER, ON THE PALACE OF
ALCINOUS, *ODYSSEY* (8TH CENTURY BC)

• • •

But come, and I will even tell thee the trees through all the terraced garden, which thou gavest me once for mine own, and I was begging of thee this and that, being but a little child, and following thee through the garden. Through these very trees we were going, and thou didst tell me the names of each of them. Pear-trees thirteen thou gavest me and ten apple-trees and figs two-score, and, as we went, thou didst name the fifty rows of vines thou wouldest give me, whereof each one ripened at divers times, with all manner of clusters on their boughs, when the seasons of Zeus wrought mightily on them from on high.

—HOMER, ODYSSEUS REMEMBERS
HIS FATHER'S GARDEN IN THE *ODYSSEY* (8TH CENTURY BC)

• • •

Judge a tree from its fruit, not from its leaves.
—EURIPIDES (5TH CENTURY BC)

• • •

What can your eye desire to see, your eares to heare, our mouth to taste, or your nose to smell, that is not to be had in an Orchard? with Abundance and Variety? . . . 1000 of Delights are in an Orchard; and sooner shall I be weary than I can reckon the least part of that pleasure which one, that hath and loves an Orchard, may find therein.

—WILLIAM LAWSON, *A NEW ORCHARD* (1618)

• • •

Apple blossoms have enhanced orchards for millennia.

A tree that takes its time in growing bears the finest fruit.
—MOLIÈRE, *THE IMAGINARY INVALID* (1673)

• • •

By a little attention to this matter, a lady with the help of her children can obtain a rich abudance of all kinds of fruit.
—CATHERINE E. BEECHER AND HARRIET BEECHER STOWE, "THE CULTIVATION OF FRUIT," *AMERICAN WOMAN'S HOME* (1869)

• • •

It is a mistake to think that because fruit-trees are useful they cannot be beautiful. How many of us, if the Apple or Peach were introduced as new flowering shrubs, would not use them gratefully in our garden schemes though they bore never a fruit.
—GRACE TABOR, *OLD-FASHIONED GARDENING: A HISTORY AND A RECONSTRUCTION* (1913)

• • •

When you work with fruit trees you are making permanent records, reaching out our hand to future generations—erecting a monument that will remain long after you are gone.
—LUTHER BURBANK, QUOTED BY HENRY THEOPHILUS FINCK, *GARDENING WITH BRAINS* (1922)

• • •

A cherry tree

Shrubs

In front of the cloister is a variegated terrace walk, with borders of box, then a descent to a sloping garden bank, with forms of animals cut out in box facing each other. On the flat ground is an acanthus so soft that I had almost called it liquid. Round this is a walk, enclosed by evergreens planted close, and cut into different shapes. Beyond this is a promenade in the form of a ring, which encircles the variously shaped boxes and the low trimmed shrubs. All this is protected by a wall covered and concealed by a flopping hedge of box.

—PLINY THE ELDER, LETTER ABOUT HIS
TUSCAN VILLA (1ST CENTURY AD)

• • •

Shrubs are, unfortunately, something you are supposed to have—marching across the front of your house like Snow White's dwarves, clipped into the usual classic shapes: the Muffin, the Golf Ball, the Chicken Croquette. . . . That's a pity, because shrubs are too versatile, and too beautiful, to be taken for granted.

—BARBARA DAMROSCH, *THE GARDENING PRIMER* (1988)

• • •

Patience is required for the yew topiary and hedges; but although it will need ten to fifteen years to reach perfection, you will be rewarded with a masterpiece.

—ROY STRONG, *SMALL PERIOD GARDENS* (1992)

• • •

A flock of topiary sheep

[A shorn hedge] signifies vision, persistence, and patience—qualities we crave in today's world. Yet many people do make the commitment. They create hedges, care for them eagerly, and gain much satisfaction from the process. Why? Perhaps it's because shaping a hedge is the closest most of us will ever come to doing sculpture or erecting a monument, but I think the real reward is more mundane. Shearing is very empowering—it gives you an exhilarating sense of control and achievement. You can stand back afterward and say, look what I've done.

—RITA BUCHANAN, "ALL ABOUT HEDGES:
HOW TO FRAME YOUR GARDEN WITH LIVING WALLS" (1999)

• • •

Vines

But the best of all climbing or rambling plants, whether for wall or arbour or pergola, is undoubtedly the grape-vine. Even when trimly pruned and trained for fruit-bearing on an outer wall it is an admirable picture of leafage and fruit-cluster; but to have it in fullest beauty it must ramp at will, for it is only when the fast-growing branches are thrown out far and wide that it fairly displays its graceful vigour and the generous magnificence of its incomparable foliage.

—GERTRUDE JEKYLL, *WOOD AND GARDEN* (1899)

• • •

To the devil with brick walls! And away too with the sedate air of those vines! Oh no, vines, you are worthy of iron arches, delicately hooped, and certainly deserving enough for me to stick supports in for you here and there, as my fancy guides me, gibbets for you to hang yourselves from, sunshades on which you can spread yourselves and droop down. . . . Vines, you shall rear yourselves into the sky, you shall breathe in the breeze that sometimes does not reach down to brush the earth, the rough undersides of your leaves shall taste the torrid mist that summer pumps up from the earth, and from your woody shoots, vines, I shall conjure myself a grove of trees.

—COLETTE, *EARTHLY PARADISE* (1966)

• • •

An arbor? Naturally I shall have an arbor. . . . I must have a trellis for my purple dragon-tongued cobaeas to perch on, and for my cane melons. . . . Cane melons? Why not a wickerwork marrow? Because the melon plant I am talking about hauls itself up the canes that are stuck up to support it, then runs between them like a green pea plant, marking every stage of its progress with little green and white melons that are very sweet and full of flavor.

—COLETTE, *EARTHLY PARADISE* (1966)

• • •

Vegetables

I have always thought a kitchen garden a more pleasant sight than the finest orangery. I love to see everything in perfection, and am more pleased to survey my rows of coleworts and cabbages, with a thousand nameless pot herbs springing up in their full fragrancy and verdure, than to see the tender plants of foreign countries.

—JOSEPH ADDISON, "GARDENS" (1712)

• • •

I used to visit and revisit it a dozen times a day, and stand in deep contemplation over my vegetable progeny with a love that nobody could share or conceive of who had never taken part in the process of creation. It was one of the most bewitching sights in the world to observe a hill of beans thrusting aside the soil, or rows of early peas just peeping forth sufficiently to trace a line of delicate green.

—NATHANIEL HAWTHORNE, *MOSSES FROM AN OLD MANSE* (1846)

• • •

Cabbage: a familiar kitchen-garden vegetable about as large and wise as a man's head.

—AMBROSE BIERCE, *THE DEVIL'S DICTIONARY* (1906)

• • •

A white asparagus making its way to the surface

A vegetable garden in the beginning looks so promising and then after all little by little it grows nothing but vegetables, nothing, nothing but vegetables.

—GERTRUDE STEIN, *WARS I HAVE SEEN* (1945)

• • •

One very easy vegetable to grow is the potato: All you do is stick a potato in the ground, and before long it germinates, and one day there is brand-new potato in exactly the same place!

—DAVE BARRY "GARDENING GROWS ON YOU,"
CHICAGO TRIBUNE (1985)

• • •

To get the best results you must talk to your vegetables.

—PRINCE CHARLES, TELEVISION INTERVIEW (1986)

• • •

Herbs

As for rosemary, I let it run all over my garden walls, not only because my bees love it but because it is the herb sacred to remembrance and to friendship, whence a sprig of it hath a dumb language.

—ATTRIBUTED TO SIR THOMAS MORE (16TH CENTURY)

• • •

A modest backyard herb garden

There's rosemary, that's for remembrance; pray you, love, remember. And there is pansies, that's for thoughts.

—WILLIAM SHAKESPEARE, *HAMLET* (1600)

. . .

Hot lavender, mints, savory, marjoram;
The marigold, that goes to bed wi' th' sun,
And with him rises weeping; these are flow'rs
Of middle summer, and I think they are given
To men of middle age.

—WILLIAM SHAKESPEARE, *WINTER'S TALE* (1610)

. . .

Those herbs which perfume the air most delightfully, not passed by as the rest, but, being trodden upon and crushed, are three; that is, burnet, wild thyme and watermints. Therefore, you are to set whole alleys of them, to have the pleasure when you walk or tread.

—FRANCIS BACON, *OF GARDENS* (1625)

. . .

Another thing worth the practicing is that you be careful to cut or top your herbs often, for it is not only handsome but causeth your herbs to last longer . . . By your often topping your sweet herbs, you may if you will, make use of them to dry and make them into powder to use all winter.

—LEONARD MEAGER, *THE ENGLISH GARDENER* (1683)

. . .

Gather herbs for drying of all sorts as are now in flower, and hang them up in a dry shady place where they may dry leisurely, which will render them better for any purpose, than if they were dried in the sun.

—PHILIP MILLER, *THE GARDENERS KALENDAR* (1732)

• • •

Much virtue in herbs, little in men.

—BENJAMIN FRANKLIN, *POOR RICHARD'S ALMANAC* (1739)

• • •

Let the mint plants, the tarragon, and the sage push up their spikes, just so high that a drooping hand, as it crushes their slender leaf stems, can set free their impatient scents. tarragon, sage, mint, savory, and burnet opening your pink flowers at noon, then closing them again three hours later, I love you certainly for yourselves—but I shall not fail to demand your presence in my salads, my stewed lamb, my seasoned sauces; I shall exploit you.

—COLETTE, *EARTHLY PARADISE* (1966)

• • •

For the best flavor, pick herbs for drying before they flower. Tie them into small bundles and hang them head downwards in a cool, dry place.

—NATIONAL TRUST, *GARDENING TIPS* (1994)

• • •

Roses

There is simply the rose; it is perfect in every moment of its existence.

—RALPH WALDO EMERSON, "SELF-RELIANCE" (1841)

• • •

But he, that dares not grasp the thorn
Should never crave the rose.

—ANNE BRONTË, "THE NARROW WAY" (1849)

• • •

A thorn defends the rose, harming only those who would steal the blossom.

—CHINESE PROVERB

• • •

I am a friend to plants; I love the rose, as the most perfect flower which our German nature can produce; but I am not fool enough to desire that my garden should produce them now, at the end of April. I am satisfied if I now find the first green leaves, satisfied if I see how one leaf after another is formed upon the stem, from week to week; I am pleased when, in May, I perceive the buds, and am happy when, at last, in June, the rose itself appears in all its splendor and all its fragrance. If any one cannot wait, let him go to the hot-houses.

—JOHANN GOETHE, CONVERSATION WITH
JOHN PETER ECKERMANN (1825)

• • •

I am passionately fond of roses, but I don't like to talk about them. The poor roses have been so abused! The Greeks said five or six pretty things about them; the Latins translated these, and added three or four of their own. From that time the poets of all countries and all ages have translated, copied, and imitated what the Greeks and Latins said, without at all heightening our love of the flower by any fresh colouring. . . . Some people are always grumbling because roses have thorns; I am thankful that thorns have roses.

—JEAN-BAPTISTE ALPHONSE KARR,
A TOUR ROUND MY GARDEN (1855)

• • •

The lily has a smooth stalk,
Will never hurt your hand;
But the rose upon her brier
Is lady of the land.

There's sweetness in an apple tree,
And profit in the corn;
But lady of all beauty
Is a rose upon a thorn.

When with moss and honey
She tips her bending brier,
And half unfolds her glowing heart,
She sets the world on fire.

—CHRISTINA ROSSETTI, "THE ROSE" (1872)

• • •

Roses can enhance any garden.

Now, a rose would smell as sweet by any other name, simply because it must still remain a rose. And a rose has its rights as well as a cabbage. The cabbage-growers say it does not pay as well as cabbage, but all the same the rose is red, and sweet, and immortal!

—ROSE ELIZABETH CLEVELAND, "JOAN OF ARC" (1885)

• • •

Our highest assurance of Providence seems to me to rest in the flowers. All other things, our powers, our desires, our food are all really necessary for our existence in the first instance. But this rose is an extra. Its smell and color are an embellishment of life, not a condition of it. It is only goodness which gives extras, and so I say again that we have much to hope from the flowers.

—ARTHUR CONAN DOYLE, "THE NAVAL TREATY,"
THE MEMOIRS OF SHERLOCK HOLMES (1894)

• • •

The splendor of the rose and the whiteness of the lily do not rob the little violet of its scent nor the daisy of its simple charm. If every tiny flower wanted to be a rose, spring would lose its loveliness.

—THÉRÈSE OF LISIEUX, *THE STORY OF A SOUL* (1895)

• • •

A perfect rose

He who would have beautiful Roses in his garden must have beautiful Roses in his heart.
—SAMUEL REYNOLDS HOLE, *A BOOK ABOUT ROSES:*
HOW TO GROW AND SHOW THEM (1896)

• • •

A rose garden may often be made much more delightful by having some point of interest besides the roses, for nothing is more usual than to find that, except in the few weeks of its fullest bloom, the rose garden is rather a dull place.
—GERTRUDE JEKYLL,
"DESIGNING A ROSE GARDEN," *THE GARDEN* (1913)

• • •

A rose is a rose is a rose is a rose.
—GERTRUDE STEIN, "SACRED EMILY" (1913)

• • •

An idealist is one who, on noticing that a rose smells better than a cabbage, concludes that it is also more nourishing.
—H. L. MENCKEN, *A LITTLE BOOK IN C MAJOR* (1916)

• • •

God gave us memory so that we might have roses in December.
—J. M. BARRIE, "COURAGE" (1922)

• • •

You are responsible, forever, for what you have tamed. You are responsible for your rose.
—ANTOINE DE SAINT-EXUPÉRY, *THE LITTLE PRINCE* (1943)

• • •

One of the most tragic things I know about human nature is that all of us tend to put off living. We are all dreaming of some magical rose garden over the horizon instead of enjoying the roses that are blooming outside our windows today.
—DALE CARNEGIE, *HOW TO STOP WORRYING
AND START LIVING* (1948)

• • •

There is nothing more difficult for a truly creative painter than to paint a rose, because before he can do so he has first to forget all the roses that were ever painted.
—HENRI MATISSE, QUOTED IN *THE NEW YORK TIMES* (1954)

• • •

Don't ask me where I shall plant the white rose disheveled by a single gust of wind, the yellow rose which has a scent of fine cigars, the pink rose which has a scent of roses, the red rose which dies unceasingly from the pouring out of its odors and whose dry and weightless corpse still lavishes its balm upon the air. I shall not crucify my red rose against a wall; I shall not bind it to the edge of the water tank. It shall grow, if my good destiny allow it so, just beside the open bedroom, the room that will have only three walls instead of four, and stand open to the rising sun.

—COLETTE, *EARTHLY PARADISE* (1966)

• • •

Show a red rose to anyone with the slightest vestige of a sense of smell, and he will automatically put his nose to it. Lacking scent, it may still make a name for itself as an exhibitor's flower, but it will touch nobody's heart.

—CHRISTOPHER LLOYD, *THE WELL-TEMPERED GARDEN* (1973)

• • •

I don't know whether nice people tend to grow roses or growing roses makes people nice.

—ROLAND A. BROWNE, *THE ROSE LOVER'S GUIDE* (1983)

• • •

CHAPTER 9

Why We Garden

He who has silver, he who has lapis lazuli, he who has oxen, and he who has sheep wait at the gate of the man who has barley.
—SUMERIAN PROVERB
(LATE 3RD/EARLY 2ND MILLENNIUM BCE)

• • •

May I wander round my pool each day forever more. May my soul sit on the branches of the grave garden I have prepared for myself. May I refresh myself each day under my sycamore.
—EGYPTIAN TOMB INSCRIPTION, THEBES (1400 BC)

• • •

Earth . . . freely offers to those that labour all things necessary
to the life of man; and, as if that were not enough, makes further contribution of a thousand luxuries. It is she who supplies
with sweetest scent and fairest show all things wherewith to
adorn the altars and statues of the gods, or deck man's person.
It is to her we owe our many delicacies of flesh or fowl or vegetable growth; since with the tillage of the soil is closely linked
the art of breeding sheep and cattle, whereby we mortals may
offer sacrifices well pleasing to the gods, and satisfy our personal needs withal.

—XENOPHON, *OECONOMICUS* V (CA. 362 BC)

• • •

This, too, is that kindliest of arts which makes requital tenfold
in kind for every work of the labourer. She is the sweet mistress
who, with smile of welcome and outstretched hand, greets the
approach of her devoted one, seeming to say, Take from me all
thy heart's desire. She is the generous hostess; she keeps open
house for the stranger. For where else, save in some happy rural
seat of her devising, shall a man more cheerily cherish content
in winter, with bubbling bath and blazing fire? or where, save
afield, in summer rest more sweetly, lulled by babbling streams,
soft airs, and tender shades?

—PLINY THE ELDER, LETTER TO GALLUS DESCRIBING
HIS LAURENTIAN VILLA (1ST CENTURY AD)

• • •

God Almighty first planted a garden. And indeed it is the purest of human pleasures. It is the greatest refreshment to the spirits of man; without which, buildings and palaces are but gross handiworks; and a man shall ever see, that when ages grow to civility and elegancy, men come to build stately sooner than to garden finely; as if gardening were the greater perfection. I do hold it, in the royal ordering of gardens, there ought to be gardens, for all the months in the year; in which severally things of beauty may be then in season.

—FRANCIS BACON, *OF GARDENS* (1625)

• • •

The Excellency of a Garden is better manifested by Experience, which is the best Mistress, than indicated by an imperfect Pen; which can never sufficiently convince the Reader of those transcendent Pleasures, that the Owner of a compleat Garden, with its magnificent Ornaments, its stately Groves, and Infinite variety of never-dying Objects of delight, every day enjoys . . . nor what an influence they have upon the Passions of the Mind, reducing a discomposed Fancy to a more sedate Temper, by contemplating on those Miracles of Nature Gardens afford.

—JOHN WOOLRIDGE, *SYSTEMA HORTICULTURAE,*
OR THE ART OF GARDENING (1677)

• • •

With a few flowers in my garden, half a dozen pictures and some books, I live without envy.

—LOPE DE VEGA (17TH CENTURY)

• • •

As gardening has been the inclination of kings and the choice of philosophers, so it has been the common favourite of public and private men; a pleasure of the greatest and the care of the meanest; and, indeed, an employment and a possession for which no man is too high nor too low.

—SIR WILLIAM TEMPLE, *UPON THE GARDENS OF EPICURUS, OR OF GARDENING IN THE YEAR 1685*

• • •

I never had any other desire so strong, and so like to covetousness, as that one which I have had always, that I might be master at last of a small house and large garden, with very moderate conveniences joined to them, and there dedicate the remainder of my life only to the culture of them and the study of nature.

—ABRAHAM COWLEY, *THE GARDEN* (1711)

• • •

A garden is the purest of human pleasures, it is the greatest refreshment to the spirits of man; without which buildings and palaces are but gross handy-works.

—WILLIAM MASON, *THE ENGLISH GARDEN: A POEM* (1767)

• • •

More grows in the garden than the gardener sows.

—OLD SPANISH PROVERB

• • •

Every emperor or ruler must, upon retiring from his official duties and audiences, have a garden in which to stroll, to look around and have rest for his heart. If he has a suitable place for this, it has a refreshing effect upon his mind and regulates his feelings, but if not, he becomes engrossed in sensual pleasures and loses his strength of will.

—EMPEROR CH'IEN-LUNG (1711–1799)

• • •

Life begins the day you start a garden.

—CHINESE PROVERB

• • •

An European will scarcely conceive my meaning, when I say, that there is scarce a garden in China which does not contain some fine moral, couch'd under the general design, where one is not taught wisdom as he walks, and feels the force of some noble truth or delicate precept resulting from the disposition of the groves, streams or grotto's.

—OLIVER GOLDSMITH, *THE CITIZEN OF THE WORLD* (1762)

• • •

To sit in the shade on a fine day, and look upon verdure, is the most perfect refreshment.

—JANE AUSTEN, *MANSFIELD PARK* (1814)

• • •

A house without a garden or orchard is unfurnished and incomplete.
—AMOS BRONSON ALCOTT, *JOURNALS (19TH CENTURY)*

• • •

In the orchard we hope to gratify the palate; in the flower garden, the eye and the smell; but in the landscape garden we appeal to that sense of the beautiful and the perfect, which is one of the highest attributes of our nature.
—ALEXANDER JACKSON DOWNING,
A TREATISE ON THE THEORY AND PRACTICE OF LANDSCAPE GARDENING, ADAPTED TO NORTH AMERICA (1841)

• • •

My garden . . . was of precisely the right extent. An hour or two of morning labor was all that it required. But I used to visit and re-visit it a dozen times a day and stand in deep contemplation over my vegetable progeny, with a love that nobody could share or conceive of, who had never taken part in the process of creation.
—NATHANIEL HAWTHORNE, *MOSSES FROM AN OLD MANSE* (1843)

• • •

Who, that has been confined to the business of the day, toiling and laboring in the "sweat of his brow," does not feel invigorated and refreshed, as he takes his walk in the cool of the evening . . . and marks the progress of his fruits and flowers?

—JOSEPH BRECK, *THE FLOWER-GARDEN, OR BRECK'S BOOK OF FLOWERS* (1851)

• • •

A morning-glory at my window satisfies me more than the metaphysics of books.

—WALT WHITMAN, "SONG OF MYSELF" (1855)

• • •

To own a bit of ground, to scratch it with a hoe, to plant seeds and watch their renewal of life—this is the commonest delight of the race, the most satisfactory thing a man can do.

—CHARLES DUDLEY WARNER, *MY SUMMER IN A GARDEN* (1870)

• • •

The glory of gardening: hands in the dirt, head in the sun, heart with nature. To nurture a garden is to feed not just on the body, but the soul.

—ALFRED AUSTIN, *THE GARDEN THAT I LOVE* (1894)

• • •

When in these fresh mornings I go into my garden before anyone is awake, I go for the time being into perfect happiness. In this hour divinely fresh and still, the fair face of every flower salutes me with a silent joy that fills me with infinite content; each gives me its color, its grace, its perfume, and enriches me with the consummation of its beauty.

—CELIA THAXTER, *AN ISLAND GARDEN* (1894)

• • •

For the love of gardening is a seed that once sown never dies, but always grows and grows to an enduring and ever-increasing source of happiness.

—GERTRUDE JEKYLL, *WOOD AND GARDEN* (1899)

• • •

It is a golden maxim to cultivate the garden for the nose, and the eyes will take care of themselves.

—ROBERT LOUIS STEVENSON, "THE IDEAL HOUSE"
FROM *ESSAYS OF TRAVEL* (1905)

• • •

There's not a pair of legs so thin, there's not a head so thick
There's not a hand so weak and white, nor yet a heart so sick
But it can find some needful job that's crying to be done
For the glory of the garden glorifieth every one.

—RUDYARD KIPLING, "THE GLORY OF THE GARDEN" (1911)

• • •

A lilac blossom pleases the nose as well as the eye.

I find the garden the greatest help and consolation in growing old.

—MARY BERENSON, LETTER TO
ISABELLA STEWART GARDNER (1912)

• • •

We can get fuel from fruit, from that shrub by the roadside, or from apples, weeds, saw-dust, almost anything! There is fuel in every bit of vegetable matter that can be fermented. There is enough alcohol in one year's yield of a hectare of potatoes to drive the machinery necessary to cultivate the field for a hundred years.

—HENRY FORD, QUOTED IN *THE NEW YORK TIMES* (1925)

• • •

I love flowers, trees, animals, and all the works of Nature as they pass before us in time and space. What a joy life is when you have made a close working partnership with Nature.

—LUTHER BURBANK, SPEECH (1926)

• • •

It is a good idea to be alone in a garden at dawn or dark so that all its shy presences may haunt you and possess you in a reverie of suspended thought.

—JAMES DOUGLAS, *DOWN SHOE LANE* (1930)

• • •

Life is a grim business but we must take refuge in the nearest task whatever it is, and dealing with gardens is one of the most helpful.

—EDITH WHARTON, LETTER TO MARY SENNI (1933)

• • •

It is utterly forbidden to be half-hearted about gardening. You have got to love your garden whether you like it or not.

—W. C. SELLAR AND R. J. YEATMAN, *GARDEN RUBBISH* (1936)

• • •

I love spring anywhere, but if I could choose I would always greet it in a garden.

—RUTH STOUT, *HOW TO HAVE A GREEN THUMB WITHOUT AN ACHING BACK* (1955)

• • •

Gardens are the link between men and the world in which they live.

—DAME SYLVIA CROWE, *GARDEN DESIGN* (1958)

• • •

Guided by my heritage of a love of beauty and a respect for strength—in search of my mother's garden, I found my own.

—ALICE WALKER, *IN SEARCH OF OUR MOTHERS' GARDENS* (1972)

• • •

There is room for many approaches to gardening and they give us the satisfaction of expressing ourselves. Ours, in its humble way, is an art as well as a craft. At the same time it keeps us in touch with the earth, the seasons and with that complex of interrelated forces both animate and inanimate, which we call nature. It is a humanizing occupation.

—CHRISTOPHER LLOYD, *THE WELL-TEMPERED GARDEN* (1978)

• • •

To create a garden is to search for a better world. In our effort to improve on nature, we are guided by a vision of paradise. Whether the result is a horticultural masterpiece or only a modest vegetable patch, it is based on the expectation of a glorious future. This hope for the future is at the heart of all gardening.

—MARINA SCHINZ, *VISIONS OF PARADISE* (1985)

• • •

I grow my own vegetables for two reasons: the quality of the crops I can produce myself, and the quality of the time I spend doing it.

—BARBARA DAMROSCH, *THE GARDEN PRIMER* (1988)

• • •

Gardening is . . . an outlet for fanaticism, violence, love, and rationality without their worst side effects.

—GEOFFREY CHARLESWORTH, *A GARDENER OBSESSED* (1994)

• • •

[My] experience in the garden leads me to believe that there are many important things about our relationship to nature that cannot be learned in the wild. For one thing, we need, and now more than ever, to learn how to use nature without damaging it. That probably can't be done as long as we continue to think of nature and culture simply as antagonists.

—MICHAEL POLLAN, *SECOND NATURE:*
A GARDENER'S EDUCATION (2003)

● ● ●

I only submit that the children of farmers are likely to know where food comes from, and that the rest of us might do well to pay attention.

—BARBARA KINGSOLVER, *ANIMAL,*
VEGETABLE, MINERAL (2008)

● ● ●

When I retire to this garden summer-house, I fancy myself a hundred miles away from my villa, and take especial pleasure in it at the feast of the Saturnalia, when, by the license of that festive season, every other part of my house resounds with my servants' mirth: thus I neither interrupt their amusement nor they my studies.

—XENOPHON, *OECONOMICUS* V (CA. 362 BC)

● ● ●

Notes on Selected Authors

Joseph Addison (1672–1719), English essayist, poet, playwright, and politician who founded *The Spectator* with Richard Steele.

Albertus Magnus (1193/1206–1280), German Dominican friar and bishop, now a Catholic saint, who was famous for his knowledge of science and for having advocated for the peaceful coexistence of science and religion.

Amos Bronson Alcott (1799–1888), an American teacher, writer, philosopher, abolitionist, and reformer; he was a good friend of Ralph Waldo Emerson and the father of Louisa May Alcott, author of *Little Women*

Jean-Baptiste Alphonse Karr (1808–1890), French critic, journalist, and novelist. After publishing several books and editing *Le Figaro*, among other journals in Paris, he went to Nice in 1855 and devoted himself to flowers.

Jean Anouil (1910–1987), French dramatist.

Aristophanes (446–ca. 386 BC), Greek comic playwright.

Reginald Arkell (1882–1959), British script writer, comic novelist, and poet.

Margaret Atwood (b. 1939), Canadian poet, novelist, literary critic, essayist, and environmental activist.

Jane Austen (1775–1817), English novelist, best known for *Pride and Prejudice* and *Emma*.

Alfred Austin (1835–1913), English poet who was appointed Poet Laureate in 1896 after the death of Alfred, Lord Tennyson.

Francis Bacon (1561–1626), English philosopher, statesman, scientist, jurist, and author.

Luis Barragán (1902–1988), Mexican architect.

J. M. Barrie (1860–1937), Scottish author and dramatist, creator of Peter Pan.

Henry Ward Beecher (1813–1887), preacher and abolitionist.

Mary Berenson, wife of art historian Bernard Berenson.

Ambrose Bierce (1842–1914), American writer, journalist, and editor.

William Blake (1757–1827), English poet, painter, and print-maker.

Barbara Dodge Borland (1904–1991), American writer and editor.

Joseph Breck (1794–1873), editor of the *New England Farmer*, one of the earliest agricultural magazines established in the United States, and founder of a firm that still sells seeds by mail order.

Anne Brontë (1820–1849), British novelist and poet, younger sister of Charlotte and Emily Brontë.

Thomas Edward Brown (1830–1897), British poet, scholar and theologian.

Comte de Buffon (Georges Louis Leclerc, 1707–1788), French naturalist, mathematician, cosmologist, encyclopedia author, and from 1739 to 1788 head of the Jardin du Roi.

Luther Burbank (1849–1926), American botanist, horticulturist, and pioneer in agricultural science.

Frances Hodgson Burnett, (1849–1924), English playwright and author, best known for her novel *The Secret Garden* (1911).

Caecilius Statius (220–ca. 166 BC), Roman comic poet.

Karel Čapek (1890–1938), Czech writer.

Dale Carnegie (1888–1955), American writer, lecturer, and the developer of famous courses in self-improvement, salesmanship, corporate training, public speaking, and interpersonal skills.

Cato the Elder (234–149 BC), Roman statesman.

Thomas Cavendish (1560–1592), English explorer and privateer.

Prince Charles (b. 1948), heir apparent to Queen Elizabeth II of England.

Geoffrey B. Charlesworth (1920–2008), British-born professor of mathematics and plantsman.

Beth Chatto (b. 1923), British plantswoman, garden designer, and author.

Emperor Ch'ien-lung (1711–1799), sixth emperor of the Manchu-led Qing dynasty.

Marcus Tullius Cicero (106–43 BC), Roman philosopher, statesman, lawyer, orator, political theorist, consul, and constitutionalist.

Rose Elizabeth Cleveland (1846–1918), First Lady of the United States during the first term of her brother, Grover Cleveland.

Colette (1873–1954), French novelist and performer.

Lucius Junius Moderatus Columella (AD 4–ca. AD 70), Roman writer on agriculture.

Abraham Cowley (1618–1667), English poet.

Dame Sylvia Crowe (1901–1997), English landscape architect and garden designer.

Emily Dickinson (1830–1886), American poet.

Diodorus Siculus (1st century BC), Greek historian.

Andrew Jackson Downing (1815–1852), American landscape designer, horticulturalist, and writer.

Arthur Conan Doyle (1859–1930), Scottish physician and writer, noted for his stories about the detective Sherlock Holmes.

Ralph Waldo Emerson (1803–1882), American essayist, lecturer, poet, and leader of the Transcendentalist movement.

John Evelyn (1620–1706), English writer, gardener, and diarist.

Henry Ford (1863–1947), American industrialist and pioneer of the assembly-line production method.

Benjamin Franklin (1706–1790), American polymath and politician, one of America's Founding Fathers.

Mahatma Gandhi (1869–1948), Hindu leader of Indian nationalism in British-ruled India.

John Gerard (1545–1611/12), English herbalist.

Johann Goethe (1749–1832), German writer, artist, and politician.

Oliver Goldsmith (1730–1774), Anglo-Irish writer and poet, best known for his novel *The Vicar of Wakefield* (1766).

Sir Henry Rider Haggard, KBE (1856–1925), English writer.

Nathaniel Hawthorne (1804–1864), American novelist and short story writer; author of such classics as *The Scarlet Letter* (1850) and *The House of Seven Gables* (1851).

Maurice Hewlett (1861–1923), English historical novelist, poet, and essayist.

James Shirley Hibberd (1825–1890), gardening writer.

Penelope Hobhouse (b. 1929), British garden writer, designer, and lecturer.

Samuel Reynolds Hole (1819–1904), Anglican priest, author, and horticulturalist.

Oliver Wendell Holmes (1809–1894), American physician, poet, professor, lecturer, and author.

Henry Home (Lord Kames) (1696–1782), Scottish advocate, judge, philosopher, writer, and agricultural improver.

Homer (mid-8th century BC), ancient Greek epic poet and author of the *Iliad* and the *Odyssey*.

Ibn Luyun (1282–1349), Spanish writer on agriculture.

Washington Irving (1783–1859), American author, essayist, biographer, travel writer, and historian.

Henry James (1843–1916), American novelist who lived most of his life in Europe.

Thomas Jefferson (1743–1826), American statesman, third president of the United States, and an active and enthusiastic gardener.

Gertrude Jekyll (1843–1932), British horticulturist, garden designer, artist, and writer.

Douglas Jerrold (1803–1857), English dramatist and writer.

Hugh Johnson (b. 1939), English wine expert and writer, also an enthusiastic gardener.

Jamaica Kincaid (b. 1949), Caribbean novelist, gardener, and gardening writer.

Barbara Kingsolver (b. 1955), American novelist, essayist, and poet.

Rudyard Kipling (1865–1936), English short-story writer, poet, and novelist.

William Lawson (d. 1635), English clergyman.

Charles Downing Lay (1877–1956), American landscape architect.

Jean Baptiste Alexandre Le Blond (1679–1719), French architect and garden designer.

Christopher Lloyd (1921–2006), British gardener and author.

John Locke (1632–1704), English philosopher and physician.

Félix Arturo Lope de Vega (1562–1635), Spanish playwright and poet.

Lucian of Samosata (ca. AD 125–after 180), Greek rhetorician and satirist.

Maurice Maeterlinck (1862–1949), Belgian playwright, poet, and essayist.

Douglas Malloch (1877–1938), American poet.

Gervase Markham (ca. 1568–1637), English poet and writer.

Andrew Marvell (1621–1678), English metaphysical poet and politician.

William Mason (1724–1797), English poet, editor, and gardener.

Henri Matisse (1869–1954), French painter.

Frederick McGourty (1936–2006), American garden designer, writer, and editor.

H. L. Mencken (1880–1956), an American journalist, essayist, magazine editor, critic, and scholar of American English.

Philip Miller (1691–1771), Scottish botanist.

Molière (1622–1673), French actor and playwright.

Claude Monet (1840–1926), French impressionist painter famed for his gardens at Giverny.

F. Frankfort Moore (1855–1931), Irish dramatist, biographer, novelist, and poet.

Sir Thomas More (1478–1535), British writer, statesman and philosopher.

William Morris (1834–1896), English textile designer, artist, writer, and libertarian socialist associated with the Pre-Raphaelite Brotherhood and the English Arts and Crafts Movement.

Samuel F. B. Morse (1791–1872), American painter, inventor who perfected the telegraph and created the garden for his home Locust Grove on Hudson River.

National Trust, British conservation organization, founded in 1895.

Frederick Law Olmsted (1822–1903), American landscape architect, best known for his design of New York City's Central Park, with Calvin Vaux.

Mirabel Osler (b. 1925), English garden writer and designer.

Russell Page (1906–1985), British gardener, garden designer, and landscape architect.

Erwin Panofsky (1892–1968), German art historian.

John Parkinson (1567–1650), the last of the great English herbalists and one of the first of the great English botanists.

Andre Parmentier (1780–1830), Belgian-born landscape architect.

Eleanor Perényi (1918–2009), American gardener and writer.

Pliny the Elder (23 AD–79 AD), Roman author, naturalist, and natural philosopher.

Edgar Allan Poe (1809–1849), American author, poet, editor, and literary critic.

Michael Pollan (b. 1955), American writer on gardening and food.

Alexander Pope (1688–1744), English poet and close friend of William Kent, prominent landscape designer of the 18th century in England.

Ramses III (1198–1167 BC), Egyptian pharaoh.

Jean Renoir (1894–1979), French film director, screenwriter, actor, producer, and author; son of the painter Pierre Renoir.

Humphry Repton (1752–1818), English landscape designer.

William Robinson (1838–1935), Irish practical gardener and journalist whose ideas about wild gardening spurred the movement that evolved into the English cottage garden.

Christina Rossetti (1830–1894), English poet.

John Ruskin (1819–1900), leading English art critic of the Victorian era, also an art patron, draftsman, watercolorist, social thinker, and philanthropist.

Vita Sackville-West (1892–1962), English author, poet, and gardener, famed for her gardens at Sissinghurt.

Antoine de Saint-Exupéry (1900–1944), French writer, poet, and pioneering aviator.

May Sarton (1912–1995), American poet, novelist, and memoirist.

Sir Walter Scott (1771–1832), English writer.

Vincent Scully (b. 1920), Sterling Professor Emeritus of the History of Art in Architecture at Yale University, and the author of many books on architecture.

W. C. Sellar (1898–1951), Scottish humorist, and **R. J. Yeatman** 1897–1968), British humorist, co-authors of *Garden Rubbish* (1936).

Seneca (ca. 4 BC–AD 65), Roman Stoic philosopher, statesman, and dramatist.

William Shakespeare (1564–1616), English poet and playwright, widely regarded as the greatest writer in the English language.

George Bernard Shaw (1856–1950), Irish playwright and a co-founder of the London School of Economics.

Henry Wheeler Shaw (1818–1885), American humorist, author of *Josh Billings: Hiz Sayings* (1865).

William Shenstone (1714–1763), English poet.

Sir George Sitwell (1860–1943), British antiquarian writer and conservative politician who sat in the House of Commons between 1885 and 1895.

Alexander Smith (1830–1867), Scottish poet.

Gertrude Stein (1874–1946), American writer, poet, feminist, and playwright, who lived most of her life in Europe.

Robert Louis Stevenson (1850–1894), Scottish novelist, poet, essayist, and travel writer.

Ruth Stout (1884–1980), American gardener and writer best known for her "No-Work" gardening books and techniques.

Walafrid Strabo (808–849), a Frankish monk and theological writer, author of *Hortulus*.

Roy Strong (b. 1935), English art historian, museum curator, writer, broadcaster, and landscape designer.

Jonathan Swift (1667–1745), Anglo-Irish satirist, essayist, political pamphleteer; author of *Gulliver's Travels* (1726).

Grace Tabor (1873–1973), American landscape architect and author.

Edwin Way Teale (1899–1980), American naturalist, photographer, and Pulitzer Prize-winning writer.

Sir William Temple (1628–1699), English statesman and essayist.

Alfred, Lord Tennyson (1809–1892), English poet.

Celia Thaxter (1835–1894), American writer of poetry and short stories.

Thérèse of Lisieux (1873–1897), French Carmelite nun.

Henry David Thoreau (1817–1862), American essayist, poet, and philosopher.

Voltaire (1694–1778), French writer, historian, and philosopher.

Alice Walker (b. 1944), American poet and activist.

Peter Walker (b. 1932), American landscape architect.

Horace Walpole (1717–1797), English art historian, antiquarian, writer, and politician.

Charles Dudley Warner (1829–1900), American essayist and novelist.

Daniel Webster (1782–1852), American statesman and senator.

Edith Wharton (1862–1937), American novelist, short story writer, and designer.

Thomas Whately (1726–1772), English politician and writer.

Katherine Whitehorn (b. 1928), British journalist, writer, and columnist.

Walt Whitman (1819–1892), American poet, essayist, and journalist.

Louise Beebe Wilder (1878–1938), American gardener and author of 20 books on gardening.

Frances Garnet Wolseley, Viscountess Wolseley (1872–1936), gardener and author.

John Woolridge (1660–1698), English agricultural writer.

William Wordsworth (1770–1850), English poet.

Frank Lloyd Wright (1867–1959), American architect, interior designer, writer, and educator.

Xenophon (ca. 430–354 BC) Greek historian, soldier, mercenary, philosopher, and writer who described life in ancient Greece and the Persian Empire and preserved the writings of Socrates. His major work *Oeconomicus* (The Economist) is a Socratic dialogue about household management and agriculture.

Works and Authors Quoted

Adams, H. S. *Making a Rock Garden*. 1912. Reprint, Whitefish, MT: Kessinger Publishing, 2010.

Adams, William Howard. *Nature Perfected: Gardens through History*. New York: Abbeville Press, 1991.

Adamson, Robert. *The Cottage Garden*, 2nd eEd. Edinburgh: Adam and Charles Black, 1856.

Addison, Joseph. "Gardens" and "Essay 477," *The Spectator* (1712). In *Essays of Joseph Addison*, vol. 1, no. 127 (1915).

Magnus, Albertus. *De Vegetabilis et Plantis* [On Vegetables and Plants], ca. 1260. Quoted in Mac Griswold, *Pleasures of the Garden*. New York: Abrams, 1988.

Alcott, Amos Bronson. *Tablets* and *Journals*, ed. Odell Shepard. Boston: Little Brown, 1938.

Allison, Christine. *365 Days of Gardening*. New York: Harper-Collins, 1995.

Anouilh, Jean. *The Lark*. New York: The Dramatists Play Service, 1952.

Aristophanes. *Peace*. Anonymous translation by the London Athenian Society, 1912. Stilwell, KS: Digireads.com, 2006.

Arkell, Reginald. "Green Fly," *Green* Fingers: A Present for a Good Gardener. Upper Saddle River, NJ: Gregg Press, 2011.

Atwood, Margaret. *Bluebeard's Egg.* Waterville, ME: Thorndike Press, 1997.

Austen, Jane. *Mansfield Park.* London: Thomas Egerton, 1814.

Austin, Alfred. *The Garden that I Love.* Macmillan & Co., 1907.

Bacon, Francis. *Of Gardens.* London, 1625.

Barragán, Luis. Official address accepting the Pritzker Architecture Prize. Washington, DC, 1980.

Barrie, J. M. "Courage" (Address delivered at St. Andrew's University on May 3, 1922).

Barry, Dave. "Gardening Grows on You (if the Grubs have Gone Fishing)," *Chicago Tribune*, June 16, 1985.

Beecher, Henry Ward. *Life Thoughts.* Boston: Phillips, Sampson and Company, 1858.

Berenson, Mary. Letter to Isabella Stewart Gardner in 1912. Quoted in May Brawley Hill, *On Foreign Soil: American Gardeners Abroad.* New York: Abrams, 2005.

Bierce, Ambrose. *The Devil's Dictionary.* New York: Neale Publishing, 1911.

Blake, William. "Proverbs of Hell," *The Marriage of Heaven and Hell.* 1793. Reprint, Oxford: Benediction Classics, 2010.

Borland, Barbara Dodge. *This is the Way My Garden Grows: And Comes into the Kitchen.* New York: W. W. Norton, 1986.

Brault, Robert. robertbrault.com.

Breck, Joseph. *The Flower-Garden, or Breck's Book of Flowers.* Boston: J. P. Jewett, 1851.

Brontë, Anne. "The Narrow Way," *Fraser's Magazine* (1849).

Brown, Thomas Edward. "My Garden," 1893. In *The Oxford Book of English Mystical Verse.* Oxford: The Clarendon Press, 1917.

Browne, Roland A. *The Rose Lover's Guide.* Reprint, New York: Board Books, 1983.

Buchanan, Rita. "All About Hedges: How to Frame Your Garden with Living Walls," *Country Living Gardener* (October 1999).

Buffon, Comte de. *Oeuvres philosophiques.* Paris, 1753.

Burbank, Luther. As quoted by Henry Theophilus Finck, *Gardening with Brains.* New York: Harper and Brothers, 1922.

Burnett, Frances Hodgson. *The Secret Garden.* New York: Grosset & Dunlap, 1911.

Caecilius Statius, quoted in *Bartlett's Familiar Quotations.* Boston: Little, Brown, 1882.

Čapek, Karel. *The Gardener's Year*, trans. M. and R. Weatherall. London, G. Allen & Unwin, 1931.

Carlisle, Carla. *South-facing Slope: Writings from "Country Life."* London: Snakeshead, 2001.

Carnegie, Dale. *How to Stop Worrying and Start Living.* London: The Chaucer Press, 1948.

Carrillo Canán, Alberto J. L. "The Gardens of Versailles and the Sublime," *Analecta Husserliana* (2003).

Cato the Elder. *De Agri Cultura* (160 BC), trans. William Davis Hooper and Harrison Boyd Ash. Cambridge, MA: Harvard University Press, 1935.

Chandogya Upanishad, 8th–7th century BC. www.dharmic-scriptures.org/Chandogya_withEnglish%28Krishnananda%29.pdf.

Charles, Prince of Wales. Interview, 1986. Referenced on BBC1's Countryfile, March 13, 2013.

Charlesworth, Geoffrey B. *The Opinionated Gardener*. Boston: David R. Godine, 1987.

_____. *A Gardener Obsessed*. Boston: David R. Godine, 1994.

Chatto, Beth. *Drought Resistant Planting through the Year*. London: Frances Lincoln, 2000.

Chatto, Beth, and Christopher Lloyd. *Dear Friend and Gardener: Letters on Life and Gardening*. London: Frances Lincoln, 1998.

Emperor Ch'ien-lung. Quoted in Mac Griswold, *Pleasures of the Garden*. New York: Abrams, 1987.

Cicero, Marcus Tullius. *Tusculanarum Disputationum*. I. 14, trans. Thomas Wilson Dougan Cambridge, UK: Cambridge University Press, 1904.

_____. Letters of Marcus Tullius Cicero, trans. E. S. Shuckburgh. London: Collier, 1910.

Cleveland, Rose Elizabeth. "Joan of Arc." In *George Eliot's Poetry: and Other Studies*. New York: Funk & Wagnalls, 1885.

Colette. *Earthly Paradise: Colette's Autobiography, drawn from the writings of her lifetime*, ed. Robert Phelps. New York: Farrar Straus, 1966.

Columella. *De Re Rustica,* trans. E. S. Forster, London: William Heinemann, 1964.

Cooke, Samuel. *The Complete English Garden, or Gardening Made Perfectly Easy*. London, 1780.

Cowley, Abraham. *The Garden*. London, 1711.

Crowe, Dame Sylvia. *Garden Design*. 1958. Reprint, Antique Collectors Club, 1958.

Damrosch, Barbara. *The Gardening Primer*. New York: Workman, 2003.

Dickinson, Emily. *Letters of Emily Dickinson*. Boston: Roberts Brothers, 1894.

Dillstone, George. *The Planning and Planting of Little Gardens*. Bedford, MA: Applewood, 1920.

Diodorus, Siculus. *Bibliotheca historica (Historical Library)*, trans. James Wellard. Newton Abbot, UK: Readers Union, 1972.

Douglas, James. *Down Shoe Lane*. London: Herbert Joseph, 1930.

Downing, Andrew Jackson. *A Treatise on the Theory and Practice of Landscape Gardening, Adapted to North America*. New York: Wiley & Putnam, 1841.

Doyle, Arthur Conan "The Naval Treaty." In *The Memoirs of Sherlock Holmes*. London, 1894.

Emerson, Ralph Waldo. "Farming." In *Society and Solitude*. Boston: Houghton Mifflin, 1870.

_____. "Man the Reformer." In *The Prose Works of Ralph Waldo Emerson*, vol. 1. Boston: James R. Osgood, 1875.

_____. *Fortune of the Republic*. Boston: Houghton, Osgood, 1878.

Evelyn, John. *Kalendarium Hortensis*. London, 1664.

Ferguson, John and Burkhard Mucke. *The Gardener's Year*. London: Frances Lincoln, 1991.

Ford, Henry. Interview, *New York Times*, 1925.

Franklin, Benjamin. *Poor Richard's Almanac*. Philadelphia, 1739.

Gandhi, Mahatma. As quoted on www.mkgandhi.org.

Gerard, John. *Herball*. London, 1597.

Glick, Thomas F. *Islamic and Christian Spain in the Early Middle Ages*. Princeton, NJ: Princeton University Press, 1979.

Goethe, Johann. "Conversation with John Peter Eckermann." In *Conversations with Eckermann and Soret*, Vol. 1. London: Smith, Elder, 1850.

Goldsmith, Oliver. *The Citizen of the World*. London, 1762.

Griswold, Mac. *Pleasures of the Garden*. New York: Abrams, 1988.

Haggard, H. Rider. *A Gardener's Year.* London: Longmans, Green, 1905.

Hawthorne, Nathaniel. *Mosses from an Old Manse.* Boston, 1843.

Hewlett, Maurice. *Open Country: A Comedy with a Sting.* New York: Charles Scribner's Sons, 1910.

Hibberd, James Shirley. *The Amateur's Flower Garden.* London: Groomsbridge and Sons, 1871; reprint 1884.

Hobhouse, Penelope. *Color in Your Garden.* Boston: Little, Brown, 1985.

Hole, Samuel Reynolds. *A Book about Roses: How to Grow and Show Them.* London and New York: E. Arnold, 1896.

Holmes, Oliver Wendell. *The Poet at the Break-Fast Table.* Boston: Houghton Mifflin, 1895.

Home, Henry. "Beauty" *Elements of Criticism*, Vol. 1. London, 1762.

Homer. *Iliad,* trans. Samuel Butler. New York: E. P. Dutton, 1925.

————. *Odyssey*, trans. Samuel Butler. New York: E. P. Dutton, 1925.

Luyun, Ibn. *Treatise on Agriculture.* Almeria, 14th century.

Irving, Washington. *The Sketchbook of Geoffrey Crayon. Gent.* New York: C.S. Van Winkle, 1819–20.

————. *Tales of the Alhambra.* New York: Lea and Carey, 1832.

James, Henry. Letter to Alice James, 1898.

Jefferson, Thomas. Letter to John Jay, 1781, and letter to Charles Willson Peale, 1811. www.let.rug.nl/usa/presidents/thomas-jefferson/letters-of-thomas-jefferson/ to John Jay in 1785.

_____. *Garden Book*, a compilation of notes from the years 1809 to 1824. https://www.masshist.org/thomasjeffersonpapers/garden/index.html.

Jekyll, Gertrude. *Wood and Garden*. London: Longmans, Green, 1899.

_____. *Home and Garden*. London: Longmans, Green, 1901.

_____. *Wall and Water Gardens*. London: Country Life, 1901.

_____. *Some English Gardens*. London: Longmans, Green, 1904.

_____. *Colour in the Flower Garden*. London: Country Life, 1908.

_____. *Colour Schemes for the Flower Garden*. London: Country Life, 1908.

_____. "Designing a Rose Garden," *The Garden* (1913).

Jerrold, Douglas. *A Land of Plenty*, 1859. Quoted in *Bartlett's Familiar Quotations*. Boston: Little Brown, 1916.

Johnson, Hugh. *Principles of Gardening*. New York: Simon & Schuster, 1997.

Karr, Jean-Baptiste Alphonse. *A Tour Round My Garden*. London: Geo. Routledge, 1855.

Kincaid, Jamaica. *My Garden (Book):*. New York: Farrar Straus, Giroux, 1999.

Kingsolver, Barbara with Steven L. Hopp and Camille Kingsolver. *Animal, Vegetable, Miracle*. New York: Harper, 2007.

Kipling, Rudyard. "The Glory of the Garden," 1911. www.kipling.org.uk/poems_garden.htm

Lawson, William. *A New Orchard*. London, 1618.

Lay, Charles Downing. *A Garden Book*. New York: Duffield, 1924.

Le Blond, Jean Baptiste Alexandre. *The Theory and Practice of Gardening*. Paris, 1712.

Lloyd, Christopher. *The Well-Tempered Garden*. London: Collins, 1973.

Locke, John. *Some Thoughts Concerning Education*. London, 1693.

Lope de Vega. As quoted in *The Best Tales from the Golden Era*. Miami: Alfaguara Juvenil, 2001.

Lucien of Samosata. *The Works of Lucian of Samosata*, Vol. 4, trans. H. W. Fowler and F. G. Fowler. Oford, UK: The Clarendon Press, 1905.

Maeterlinck, Maurice. *The Intelligence of the Flower*. New York: Dodd Mead, 1907.

Malloch, Douglas. "Whoever Makes a Garden." In *American Lumberman* (ca. 1900).

Markham, Gervase. *The English Husbandman*. London, 1613.

Martin, Mitra K. "*In Search of Paradise*," *Analecta Husserliana* (2003).

Martineau, Mrs. Philip. *The Secrets of Many Gardens*. New York: D. Appleton, 1924.

Marvell, Andrew. *Upon Appleton House*. London, early 1650s.

Matisse, Henri. "Obituary," *New York Times*, November 4, 1954.

McGourty, Frederick. *The Perennial Gardener*. Boston: Houghton Mifflin, 1989.

Meager, Leonard. *The Complete English Gardener*. London, 1670.

Mencken, H. L. *A Little Book in C Major*. New York: John Lane, 1916.

Miller, Philip. *The Gardeners Kalendar*. London, 1732.

Mitchell, Henry. *The Essential Earthman: Henry Mitchell on Gardening*. Bloomington, IN: Indiana University Press, 1981.

Moliere. *The Imaginary Invalid*, trans. Miles Malleson. London: Samuel French, 1959.

Monet, Claude. Quoted on *www.claudemonet.com*

Moore, F. Frankfort. *A Garden of Peace*. New York: George H. Doran, 1919.

Morris, William. *Making the Best of It. A paper read before Tile Trades' Guild of Learning and the Birmingham Society of Artists*, 1879.

_____. "Gossip about an Old House." *The Quest* (1895).

Morse, Samuel F. B. *Lectures on the Affinity of Painting with the Other Fine Arts*. New York, 1826.

Lady Murasaki. *Tale of Genji*, trans. Arthur Waley. Boston: Houghton Mifflin, 1934.

National Trust. *Gardening Tips*. London: National Trust, 1994.

Olmsted, Frederick Law. *The Spoils of the Park*. New York: 1882.

Osler, Mirabel. *A Gentle Plea for Chaos*. New York: Arcade, 1989.

Page, Russell. *The Education of a Gardener*. New York: Atheneum, 1962.

Panofsky, Erwin. "The Ideological Antecedents of the Rolls-Royce Radiator." *Proceedings of the American Philosophical Society 107 (1963).*

Parkinson, John. *A Garden of Pleasant Flowers*. London, 1629.

Parmentier, André. "Landscapes and Picturesque Gardens." *The New American Gardener* (1828).

Perényi, Eleanor. *Green Thoughts*. New York: Random House, 1981.

Pliny the Younger. *Letters*, trans. John Delaware Lewis. London: Kegan Paul, Trench, Trübner, 1890.

Poe, Edgar Allan." The Landscape Garden." Ladies Companion (October 1842).

Pollan, Michael. Second Nature: *A Gardener's Education*. New York: Grove/Atlantic, 1991.

Pope, Alexander. *The Complete Works of Alexander Pope*. London: John Murray, 1889.

Renoir, Jean. *My Life and My Films*. New York: Da Capo Press, 1974.

Repton, Humphry. *The landscape gardening and landscape architecture of the late Humphrey Repton, esq.* London, 1840.

Robinson, William. *The Wild Garden*. London: John Murray, 1870.

————. *The English Flower Garden*. London: John Murray, 1883.

Rossetti, Christina. *Christina Rossetti: The Complete Poems*. London: Penguin Books, 2001.

Ruskin, John. *Modern Painters*, vol. 3. London, 1856.

Sackville-West, Vita. *The Dark Island*. Garden City, NY: Doubleday Doran, 1934.

————. *In Your Garden*. London: Michael Joseph, 1949.

————. *More for Your Garden*. London: Michael Joseph, 1953.

————. *Vita Sackville West's Garden Book*. London: Michael Joseph, 1968.

Saint-Exupéry, Antoine de. *The Little Prince,* trans. Katherine Woods. New York: Reynal and Hitchcock, 1943.

Sakuteiki. *Visions of the Japanese Garden,* 11th century. Quoted in Marc Peter Keane and Haruzō Ōhashi, *Japanese Garden Design*. Rutland, VT: 1997.

Sarton, May. *Plant Dreaming Deep*. New York: Norton, 1984.

Schinz, Marina. *Visions of Paradise*. New York: Stewart, Tabori & Chang, 1985.

Scott, Sir Walter. "On Landscape Gardening," *Quarterly Review* (1828).

Scully, Vincent. *Modern Architecture and Other Essays*. Princeton, NJ: Princeton University Press, 2007.

Sedding, John Dando. *Garden-Craft Old and New*. London: John Lane, The Bodley Head, 1891.

Sellar, W. C. and R. J. Yeatman. *Garden Rubbish*. New York: Farrar & Rinehart, 1936.

Seneca the Younger. *The Epistles of Lucas Annaeus Seneca*. London: W. Woodfall, 1786.

Shakespeare, William. *Love's Labours Lost*. London, 1594–95.

_____. King Henry VI, Part 2. London, 1596–99.

_____. *Hamlet*. London, 1600.

_____. *Winter's Tale*. London, 1610.

Shaw, George Bernard. *The Adventures of the Black Girl in Her Search for God*. London: Constable, 1932.

Shaw, Henry Wheeler. *Josh Billings: Hiz Sayings*. New York: G. W. Carleton, 1865.

Shenstone, William. "Interview," 1746. Quoted in *The Works in Verse and Prose of William Shenstone, Esq*. London: R. and R. Dodsley, 1746.

Sidgwick, Cecily Ullmann. *The Children's Book of Gardening.* New York: Macmillan, 1909.

Sitwell, Sir George. *On the Making of Gardens.* London: John Murray, 1909.

Smith, Alexander. *Books and Gardens.* London, 1863.

Stein, Gertrude. *Selected Writings of Gertrude Stein.* New York: Vintage Books, 1990.

Stevenson, Robert Louis. "The Ideal House," *Essays of Travel.* London: Chatto & Windus, 1905.

Stout, Ruth. *How to Have a Green Thumb without an Aching Back.* New York: Galahad Books, 1955.

Strabo, Walafrid. *Hortulus,* trans. Raef Payne. Pittsburgh: Carnegie Mellon Press, 1966.

Strong, Roy. *Small Period Gardens.* New York: Rizzoli, 1992.

Sumerian proverbs and text. In ETCSL project, Faculty of Oriental Studies, University of Oxford.

Swanwick, Helena. *The Small Town Garden.* Manchester, UK, 1907.

Tabor, Grace. *Old-Fashioned Gardening: A History and a Reconstruction.* New York: McBride, Nast & Company, 1913.

Teale, Edwin Way. *Autumn Across America.* New York: Dodd Mead, 1956.

Temple, Sir William. *Upon the Gardens of Epicurus, or of Gardening in the Year 1685.* London, 1685.

Tennyson, Alfred Lord. "Amphion," 1842. In *The Works of Alfred, Lord Tennyson*. London: Macmillan, 1903.

Thaxter, Celia. *An Island Garden*. Boston: Houghton Mifflin, 1894.

Thérèse of Lisieux. *Story of a Soul*. London, 1895.

Voltaire. *Candide*. Paris, 1759.

Walker, Alice. *In Search of Our Mothers' Gardens*. New York: Harcourt Brace, 1972.

Walker, Peter. *Minimalist Gardens*. Washington DC: Spacemaker Press, 1996.

Walpole, Horace. "History of the Modern Taste in Gardening," *Anecdotes of Painting in England*, vol. 4. London: 1782.

Warner, Charles Dudley. *My Summer in a Garden*. Boston: Houghton Mifflin, 1870.

Webster, Daniel. *Remarks on Agriculture*. Boston, 1840.

Weston, Ezra. *Lecture at Massachusetts Horticultural Society in 1845*. Quoted in Michael Pollan, *Second Nature: A Gardener's Education*. New York: Grove Press, 1991.

Wharton, Edith. *Italian Villas and Their Gardens*. New York: The Century Company, 1905.

_____. Edith Wharton to Mary Senni, 1933.

Whateley, Thomas. *Observations on Modern Gardening*. London, 1770.

Whitehorn, Katherine. *Observations*. London: Methuen, 1970.

Whitman, Walt. "Song of Myself" and "Give Me the Splendid Sun." In *Leaves of Grass*. Brooklyn, 1855.

Wilder, Louise Beebe. *Colour in My Garden*. Garden City, NY: Doubleday, 1918.

Wiley, Keith. *Shade: Ideas and Inspiration for Shady Gardens*. Portland, OR: Timber Press, 2007.

Wilson, Helen Van Pelt. *The New Perennials Preferred*. New York: Collier Books, 1992.

Wolseley, Frances. *Gardening for Women*. London: Cassell, 1908.

Woolridge, John. *Systema Horticulturae, or the Art of Gardening*. London, 1677.

Wordsworth, William. *Of Building and Gardening and Laying Out of Grounds*. London, 1805.

Wright, Frank Lloyd. *An Autobiography*. London: Longmans, Green, 1932.

Xenophon. *Oeconomicus*, trans. H. G. Dakyns. London and New York, 1890–97.